W9-BWX-204

Life in the Time of Shakespeare

Hal Marcovitz

San Diego, CA

© 2015 ReferencePoint Press, Inc.
Printed in the United States

For more information, contact:
ReferencePoint Press, Inc.
PO Box 27779
San Diego, CA 92198
www.ReferencePointPress.com

ALL RIGHTS RESERVED.
No part of this work covered by the copyright hereon may be reproduced or used in any form or by any means—graphic, electronic, or mechanical, including photocopying, recording, taping, web distribution, or information storage retrieval systems—without the written permission of the publisher.

LIBRARY OF CONGRESS CATALOGING-IN-PUBLICATION DATA

Marcovitz, Hal.
  Life in the time of Shakespeare / by Hal Marcovitz.
    pages cm. — (Living history series)
  Includes bibliographical references and index.
  ISBN-13: 978-1-60152-778-3 (hardback)
  ISBN-10: 1-60152-778-0 (hardback)
  1. Great Britain—Social life and customs—16th century—Juvenile literature. 2. Great Britain—History—Elizabeth, 1558–1603—Juvenile literature. 3. Great Britain—History—Tudors, 1485–1603—Juvenile literature. I. Title.
  DA355.M323 2014
  942.05'5—dc23
                                                            2014027004

Contents

Foreword   4

Important Events in the Time of Shakespeare   6

Introduction   8
  Afternoons at the Globe Theatre

Chapter One   12
  The Queen and Her Court

Chapter Two   27
  Language and Learning in Shakespeare's Day

Chapter Three   41
  City Life and Country Life

Chapter Four   57
  Crime and Punishment

Chapter Five   71
  Life at Sea

Source Notes   85

For Further Research   89

Index   91

Picture Credits   95

About the Author   96

Foreword

History is a complex and multifaceted discipline that embraces many different areas of human activity. Given the expansive possibilities for the study of history, it is significant that since the advent of formal writing in the Ancient Near East over six thousand years ago, the contents of most nonfiction historical literature have been overwhelmingly limited to politics, religion, warfare, and diplomacy.

Beginning in the 1960s, however, the focus of many historical works experienced a substantive change worldwide. This change resulted from the efforts and influence of an ever-increasing number of progressive contemporary historians who were entering the halls of academia. This new breed of academician, soon accompanied by many popular writers, argued for a major revision of the study of history, one in which the past would be presented from the ground up. What this meant was that the needs, wants, and thinking of ordinary people should and would become an integral part of the human record. As British historian Mary Fulbrook wrote in her 2005 book, *The People's State: East German Society from Hitler to Honecker,* students should be able to view "history with the people put back in." This approach to understanding the lives and times of people of the past has come to be known as social history. According to contemporary social historians, national and international affairs should be viewed not only from the perspective of those empowered to create policy but also through the eyes of those over whom power is exercised.

The American historian and best-selling author, Louis "Studs" Terkel, was one of the pioneers in the field of social history. He is best remembered for his oral histories, which were firsthand accounts of everyday life drawn from the recollections of interviewees who lived during pivotal events or periods in history. Terkel's first book, *Division Street America* (published in 1967), focuses on urban living in and around Chicago and is a compilation of seventy interviews of immigrants and native-born Americans. It was followed by several other oral histories including *Hard Times* (the 1930s depression), *Working* (people's feelings about their jobs), and his 1985 Pulitzer Prize–winning *The Good War* (about life in America before, during, and after World War II).

In keeping with contemporary efforts to present history by people and about people, ReferencePoint's *Living History* series offers students a journey through recorded history as recounted by those who lived it. While modern sources such as those found in *The Good War* and on radio and TV interviews are readily available, those dating to earlier periods in history are scarcer and often more obscure the further back in time one investigates. These important primary sources are there nonetheless waiting to be discovered in literary formats such as posters, letters, and diaries, and in artifacts such as vases, coins, and tombstones. And they are also found in places as varied as ancient Mesopotamia, Charles Dickens's England, and Nazi concentration camps. The *Living History* series uncovers these and other available sources as they relate the "living history" of real people to their student readers.

Important Events in

1558
On November 17 Queen Mary dies; her half sister, Queen Elizabeth I, ascends to the throne of England.

1564
William Shakespeare is born in the village of Stratford-upon-Avon.

1553
Queen Mary ascends to the throne of England.

1577
Sir Francis Drake sets sail on a circumnavigation of the world.

1531
English philosopher Thomas Elyot publishes the essay *The Governour* in which he calls for formal education for the aristocracy.

| 1500 | 1520 | 1540 | 1560 | 1580 |

1533
Henry VIII divorces Catherine of Aragon and marries Anne Boleyn, setting off a dispute with the Catholic Church that culminates a year later with the establishment of the Church of England. The couple's daughter, Elizabeth, is born on September 7.

1568
Mary Stuart, queen of Scotland, is overthrown by Protestant nobles. Seeking refuge in England, Mary is instead imprisoned by her half sister Elizabeth.

1485
The Wars of the Roses conclude, establishing the House of Tudor as the ruling dynasty in England.

1586
Queen Elizabeth's master spy, Sir Francis Walsingham, uncovers a plot to overthrow the queen. Catholic noble Anthony Babington and thirteen conspirators are drawn and quartered. Walsingham also implicates Mary Stuart in the plot, and she is executed in 1587.

the Time of Shakespeare

1588
The English fleet under the command of Drake and Lord Charles Howard defeats the Spanish armada off the coast of France.

1604
Schoolmaster Robert Cawdrey publishes the first English language dictionary, *A Table Alphabeticall.*

1610
Henry Hudson sets sail to find the Northwest Passage through Arctic waters; his crew mutinies and Hudson is never seen again.

1603
Elizabeth I dies; having never married and given birth to an heir, she is succeeded by James I, the son of Mary Stuart.

1590   1595   1600   1605   1610

1596
Sir John Harrington, godson of the queen, invents history's first flush toilet; Harrington is ridiculed and the toilet never goes into production, but history eventually recognizes his invention by giving the nickname "john" to commodes.

1607
The first permanent colony in America is established by English settlers at Jamestown, Virginia.

1598
The Globe Theatre in London produces its first play; the theater becomes the primary venue for Shakespeare's plays.

1616
On April 23 Shakespeare dies at Stratford-upon-Avon.

Introduction

Afternoons at the Globe Theatre

Playwright and poet William Shakespeare's England was a land of contrasts: The wealthiest people lived in grand countryside estates or luxurious mansions in London's most fashionable neighborhoods, found in the western half of the city. They dined on fine meats and sipped expensive wines. They employed servants. Their clothes reflected their wealth: Women wore colorful hand-sewn gowns made of expensive fabrics; men wore frilly high-collared shirts, hats decorated with feathers, and tightly tailored trousers known as canions. The wealthiest aristocrats were likely to serve in Parliament, where they enacted laws and advised the queen.

The poorest denizens of Shakespeare's England lived much different lives. In the country they lived on farms in modest dwellings with thatched roofs and dirt floors. Whole families shared these tiny cottages. In the London of the sixteenth and seventeenth centuries, poor people resided in cramped quarters on the western side of the city. If they were able-bodied, they may have lived and worked in London's workhouses, often sponsored by neighborhood churches, where they earned meager wages making cloth. Others lived on the streets, making their way through life as beggars or thieves.

> **WORDS IN CONTEXT**
>
> **workhouses**
>
> Places of employment and residency, usually sponsored by local churches, in which people were provided jobs, small incomes, and modest lodgings.

Regardless of whether an Englishman or Englishwoman was rich or poor, at three o'clock on a summer afternoon many could be found at London's Globe Theatre, where Shakespeare's plays were performed. The octagon-shaped theater, which produced its first play in 1598, could accommodate as many as three thousand spectators. The Globe was an outdoor theater. Those who could afford seats sat in the shade under thatched awnings. Those who could not—spectators known as groundlings—paid

In this artist's rendering, Shakespeare performs at the Globe Theatre. The open-air Globe could hold as many as three thousand people during a performance.

a mere penny for admission; they stood below the stage in a dusty central area. It was not unusual for the groundlings to be more concerned with their card games and gambling than with the story unfolding on the stage. On the hottest of summer days—perhaps on a day when a much-anticipated Shakespearean play premiered—the unwashed groundlings packed shoulder-to-shoulder below the stage were known to those in the seats as stinkards. Wrote Stephen Gosson, an aristocrat, poet, and essayist of the era, "In our assemblies at plays in London, you shall see such heaving and shoving, such itching and shouldering . . . [women take] such care in their garments that they be not trod on . . . such pillows to their backs, that they take no hurt . . . such toying, such smiling, such winking . . . that it is a right comedy to mark their behavior."[1]

> **WORDS IN CONTEXT**
>
> **groundlings**
> Theater attendees who paid the minimum price for admission; they stood in open central areas of the Globe and other theaters.

Shakespeare's Plays

Whether they sat among the aristocrats under the thatched awnings, or stood among the stinkards, theatergoers were treated to the work of a writer regarded as history's finest dramatist. During his lifetime, from 1564 to 1616, Shakespeare authored thirty-eight plays as well as many other works, particularly his poetic sonnets. His plays fall into three categories: tragedies, comedies, and histories. As their descriptions suggest, Shakespeare's tragedies invariably ended sadly in the deaths of the main characters, often falling victim to their own misdeeds. On the other hand, the comedies were sheer fun, packed with irony, misunderstandings, pompous characters, and slapstick. Moreover, Shakespeare populated his stage with many fantastical characters: witches, ghosts, fairies, and others from the supernatural world. Comparing a Shakespearean play to the art of fine sailing, the seventeenth-century English historian Thomas Fuller wrote, "Shakespeare . . . could turn with all the tides, tack about, and take advantage of all winds by the quickness of his wit and invention."[2]

Some of Shakespeare's plays are entirely fictitious, such as the fantasy *A Midsummer Night's Dream* or the spoof-like *Much Ado About Nothing*; others were based on historical figures or events, such as *Julius Caesar* or *Richard III*. Romance was often a factor in Shakespeare's plays—the tragedy *Romeo and Juliet* serves as the most famous example of Shakespeare's romanticism.

In his day Shakespeare's plays were performed by England's finest actors—among them Richard Burbage, Robert Armin, Nathan Field, Edward Alleyn, and William Kemp. Women would not take the stage in England until 1660—until then the profession of acting was regarded as unladylike. Therefore, during Shakespeare's lifetime the parts of female characters were often played by teenage boys. Shakespeare himself occasionally played roles in the Globe's productions—he is believed to have taken on the role of the ghost in the tragedy *Hamlet*.

The Elizabethan Era

Shakespeare's plays were a significant element of the culture of England in the late sixteenth and early seventeenth centuries. Those years are known as the Elizabethan era, so named for Queen Elizabeth I, who ruled during much of Shakespeare's lifetime. It was Elizabeth, an enormously popular monarch, who guided England through prosperous times, made her country into a great maritime and military power, and influenced the culture of her nation. Elizabeth created the type of environment in which her talented subjects, Shakespeare foremost among them, could let their creativity flourish, spreading the culture of England beyond British shores and eventually to the New World.

Chapter One

The Queen and Her Court

She rode through the streets of London on November 28, 1558, clad in the purple velvet gown of royalty, her procession consisting of some one thousand attendants and soldiers. Tens of thousands of Londoners lined the streets, cheering wildly as her carriage passed by. "God save Queen Elizabeth!"[3] was shouted over and over again. Ironically, the procession led past the somber Tower of London, where she had been imprisoned awaiting execution four years earlier—falsely accused of plotting to overthrow her half sister, Queen Mary.

Eleven days earlier, Mary had died at age forty-two—probably a victim of influenza. Widely despised by many of her subjects—they dubbed her "Bloody Mary"—she was notorious for her persecution and execution of Protestants. On the day of Mary's death, a courier rode the 36 miles (58 km) north of London to Elizabeth's castle in Hatfield to announce the passing of the monarch and the declaration that Elizabeth was now queen of England.

Elizabeth promised the English people of Shakespeare's time that they would experience a much different reign from her than what had occurred under Mary. She dedicated herself to uniting her people and creating a society in which the ideas of the European Renaissance—an era of great advances in the arts, sciences, and literature—could flourish. On the day of her coronation, she told her subjects, "Be ye ensured that I will be as good unto you as ever Queen was unto her people. No will in me can lack, neither do I trust shall there lack any power. And persuade yourselves that for the safety and quietness of you all I will not spare if need be to spend my blood."[4]

On the day she was crowned queen of England, Elizabeth was just twenty-five years old. She ruled for nearly a half century.

The House of Tudor

Elizabeth's ascension to the throne of England had its roots in the Wars of the Roses, a series of civil wars fought in England between 1455 and 1485. The enemies were two aristocratic families, or houses, each laying claim to the English throne: the Houses of York and Lancaster. The conflicts acquired their name by the emblems of each house: a red rose for Lancaster, a white rose for York.

Shakespeare wrote about the Wars of the Roses in three of his plays, most notably the history *Richard III*. The protagonist of the play, King Richard III, was the last monarch of the House of York. Shakespeare portrays the hunchbacked Richard as a despotic, mad, and evil ruler. In Shakespeare's play Richard admits to exerting his rule through deceitful measures, claiming to be a pious man:

> And thus I clothe my naked villainy
> With odd old ends stol'n forth of holy writ,
> And seem a saint when most I play the devil.[5]

Richard met his death at the Battle of Bosworth of 1485, which ended the Wars of the Roses and resulted in the ascendancy to the throne of Henry Tudor, a member of the House of Lancaster. The new monarch, who ruled England as Henry VII, united the two warring houses by marrying Elizabeth of York, a niece of Richard III. Henry also established the House of Tudor, a dynasty that ruled England for more than a century.

Era of Turmoil

In the seventy-three years between the death of Richard III and the coronation of Elizabeth, England was a place of turmoil, revolution, and persecution. Upon his death in 1509, Henry VII was succeeded by his son, Henry VIII, who defied the authority of the Roman Catholic Church—a significant influence in the lives of most Europeans of the era.

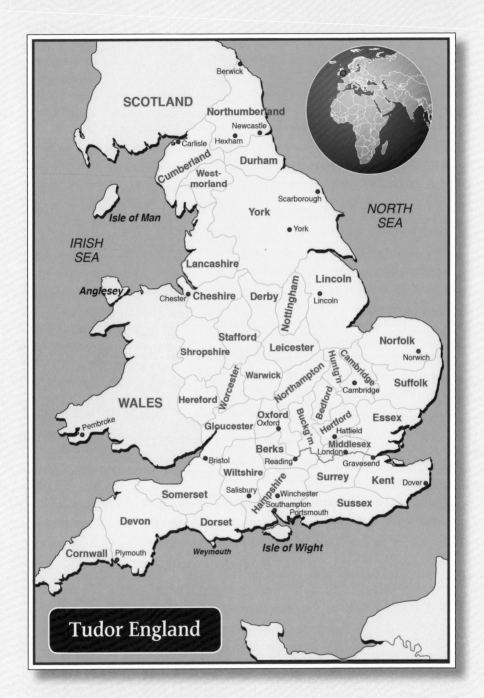

Tudor England

Henry's anger with the Catholic Church stemmed from an affair of the heart. He married Catherine of Aragon—the daughter of the king of Spain—at age seventeen, but by the time he reached his forties Henry found himself infatuated with Anne Boleyn, the daughter of an aristocrat. He was also concerned with Catherine's inability to provide him with a male heir; his union with Catherine had produced a single daughter—the future queen Mary. When Pope Clement VII refused to grant Henry permission to divorce Catherine, the king declared that he did not need papal permission. He divorced Catherine and married Anne in January 1533, and a year later, at his behest, Parliament passed laws creating the Church of England and recognizing the king—not the pope—as the head of the church.

This was the beginning of the Protestant Reformation in England, a movement that had been led in Germany by Martin Luther and in France by John Calvin. Both men questioned the supreme judgment of the pope to define the practice of Christianity. Luther, Calvin, and other reformers argued that more power to interpret the Christian Bible should be placed in the hands of local ministers. The Reformation sparked widespread discord throughout Europe as the popes sought to maintain their authority and, relying on the loyalty of Catholic monarchs, waged war against the reformers.

> **WORDS IN CONTEXT**
> **Reformation**
> The era in which Protestant churches were formed, breaking away from the authority of the Roman Catholic Church.

Bloody Mary

On September 7, 1533, Anne gave birth to Elizabeth—the only child produced through her union to Henry. By 1536 Henry's eye had wandered once more. He accused Anne of treason and had her beheaded in the Tower of London. As for Henry, the king married four more times. It was his third wife, Jane Seymour, who in 1537 blessed Henry with a male heir.

Henry died in 1547 and was succeeded by his son, Edward VI, who took the throne at age nine. Edward was a sickly child and died at age fifteen. (During the boy's brief reign, a group of adult advisors, the Council of Regency, guided the young monarch.) Henry's will decreed that he should be succeeded by a male heir, and if none existed, he designated Mary as his first heir, to be followed by Elizabeth. Soon after Edward's death, Mary was crowned queen on July 19, 1553.

Born Catholic, Mary aimed to put an end to the Protestant Reformation in England. She appointed a representative of the pope as spiritual leader of the Church of England, a position known as the archbishop of

Canterbury. Moreover, during her reign Mary had hundreds of Protestant leaders beheaded or burned at the stake—a reign of terror that earned her the nickname Bloody Mary. In 1563, five years after Mary's death, the English historian John Foxe wrote, "We earnestly pray that the annals of no country, Catholic or pagan, may ever be stained with such a repetition of human sacrifices to papal power, and that the detestation in which the character of Mary is holden may be a beacon to succeeding monarchs to avoid the rocks of fanaticism!"[6]

Elizabeth narrowly escaped the wrath of her half sister. Soon after taking the throne, Mary announced plans to marry Prince Phillip, the successor to the king of Spain—a country ardently devoted to Catholicism. Fearing a Catholic takeover of their country, in 1554 a group of Protestant nobles led by Sir Thomas Wyatt led a rebellion aimed at deposing Mary and installing Elizabeth as queen. The Wyatt rebellion was prompted largely by the fears of aristocrats that they would lose large tracts of valuable land that had been awarded to them by Henry who, after creating the Church of England, stripped the Catholic Church of its English properties. Mary successfully put down the rebellion; she had Elizabeth imprisoned in the Tower, accused of complicity in the rebellion.

Mary wanted Elizabeth executed but was talked out of her plans by Phillip. Knowing that the daughter of Henry VIII was popular among the English people and fearing a major uprising against Catholics in England should the Protestant Elizabeth be executed, Phillip convinced Mary to release Elizabeth. For good measure, though, Mary had Elizabeth placed under house arrest and kept under watch in the countryside at the castle in Hatfield. After four years of virtual exile at Hatfield, Elizabeth succeeded her half sister as queen.

Politics and Spinsterhood

Although Henry's will designated Mary and Elizabeth as heirs to his throne, Henry expected—as did many in the English aristocracy of the era—that in the event either of his daughters took the throne, they would find husbands who would hold the true authority in the royal house. In sixteenth-century England, women were not envisioned as leaders of nations. In 1545 the English philosopher Thomas Elyot wrote, "In the partes of wisdom and civile policy, [women] be founden unapt, and to

In Their Own Words

Promising Fair and Prosperous Rule

Two days after learning that she had ascended to the throne of England following the death of her half sister Mary, Elizabeth prepared to leave her castle in Hatfield for the 36-mile (58 km) trip to London. On November 19, 1558, many members of the aristocracy as well as commoners gathered at Hatfield to see the new queen off on her journey. Before embarking on her ride to London, the queen spoke to her assembled subjects, calling on their assistance to ensure her rule would be fair and her people prosperous:

> My Lords: the laws of nature move me to sorrow for my sister; the burden that has fallen upon me maketh me amazed; and yet, considering I am God's creature ordained to obey His appointment, I will thereto yield; desiring from the bottom of my heart that I may have assistance of His grace to be the minister of His heavenly will in the office now committed to me. And as I am not but one body materially considered, though by His permission a body politic to govern, so shall I desire you all, my lords, chiefly you of the nobility, every one in his degree and power, to be assistant to me; that I with my ruling, and you with your service, may make a good account to Almighty God, and leave some comfort to our posterity on earth.

Quoted in Will Durant, *The Age of Reason Begins: The Story of Civilization*, vol. 7. New York: Simon & Schuster, 1961, p. 3.

Queen Elizabeth I, who ascended the throne in 1558, was the monarch of England during much of Shakespeare's lifetime. During her reign, the nation became a place where the creativity of individuals like Shakespeare could flourish.

have litell capacite."[7] In fact, after her marriage to Phillip, Mary handed all matters of foreign diplomacy over to her husband.

But Elizabeth never married, a decision based partly on personal fears and partly on politics. Although she was expected to provide an heir to the throne, it is likely that Elizabeth feared pregnancy because the death of mothers during childbirth was a common occurrence in the sixteenth century. Two of her father's wives died in childbirth; so had many of Elizabeth's friends. (Even so, Elizabeth was known throughout her long reign to have carried on affairs with nobles—most famously with Robert Dudley, Earl of Leicester. She even insisted, until her death, that she had remained a virgin, but her closest friends and advisors suspected otherwise.)

But politics was also responsible for Elizabeth's lifelong spinsterhood. Her half sister's marriage to the future Spanish king, a Catholic, had angered many of her subjects. Therefore, a union with another European monarch—virtually all of whom were Catholics—was sure to provoke similar animosities by the English aristocrats. They feared a return to state-sanctioned Catholicism as well as the loss of lands awarded to them by Henry VIII. Moreover, there is no question that had she married she would have been forced, through tradition, to cede her authority to her husband. "I know I have the body of a weak and feeble woman," she once declared, "but I have the heart and stomach of a King."[8]

An Authoritarian Monarch

Elizabeth was authoritarian, bullying the Parliament to pass her laws and accept her policies. In the sixteenth century such absolutism was accepted by both the aristocracy and the commoners. And she was no more hesitant to toss her enemies in the Tower of London than her half sister had been. The aristocrat John Hayward, who spent a year in the Tower when Elizabeth suspected him of treason, nevertheless remained very respectful of his queen. "If any person had eyther the gift or the stile to winne the hearts of people, it was the Queene,"[9] he wrote.

> **WORDS IN CONTEXT**
> **heretic**
> In the eyes of the Catholic church, anyone who did not accept the pope as supreme authority over Christianity or who dissented from church teachings.

Moreover, even though roughly half her subjects were still devoted Catholics, they accepted her as their monarch. William Cecil, her top advisor, was a Catholic. And in Rome even the pope, Sixtus V, professed a grudging admiration for Elizabeth: "If she were not a heretic," Sixtus said, "she would be worth the whole world."[10] Keeping her people's taxes low also may have helped her gain their devotion, although during her reign the English government's treasury was habitually short of funds.

The Privy Council

Elizabeth may have been the unquestioned and supreme ruler of England, but she relied on many close advisors to help guide her decisions. Cecil was her most valued advisor, but there were others—members of an administrative body known as the Privy Council. Elizabeth appointed all the members and made sure to keep the membership small. Mary had appointed fifty members to her Privy Council, but Elizabeth saw how infighting among the council members often led to dissent, so she reduced council membership to nineteen.

WORDS IN CONTEXT
Privy Council
Council of top advisors to the queen, composed of aristocrats.

The council, composed of members of the aristocracy, did a fair amount of governing. Council members dealt with matters the queen delegated to them; among these duties were administration of the army and navy, relations with the archbishop of Canterbury, and regulation of banks. The Privy Council issued proclamations in the queen's name. Often, when Elizabeth called the council into session to hear their ideas on a knotty issue, she received contradictory advice from members—a situation she encouraged. Elizabeth believed that a divided council made her stronger. The council, for example, many times reported to her its unanimous decision that she should take a husband. When Elizabeth asked the council to nominate a candidate, the council's decision was never unanimous—a situation Elizabeth exploited by declaring that she would never marry until the Privy Council could find unanimous agreement on a suitor. The Privy Council could never agree, and Elizabeth never married.

For much of Elizabeth's reign the head of the Privy Council was Cecil, whose official title was secretary of state. After Cecil's death in 1598, he was succeeded by Sir Francis Walsingham, a very close ally who had created a vast and effective spy network—key to rooting out insurgencies in England as well as learning the plans of foreign adversaries.

Looking Back

Why Elizabeth Never Married

Elizabeth never married, thus holding sole authority in England for nearly a half century—a most unusual phenomenon during an era when women were not regarded as leaders or capable of holding political office. According to Jo McMurtry, professor of English at the University of Richmond in Virginia, Elizabeth's reasons for remaining unmarried were both personal and political:

> From a dynastic point of view, Queen Elizabeth seemed made to order. She was young—twenty-five—when she came to the throne, healthy, intelligent, and devoted to her country. Surely she would marry . . . strengthening England's international alliances while so doing, and ensure the future by leaving an heir.
>
> But the Queen did not marry. Explanations vary. International diplomacy involved many delicate balances of power and to conduct tentative negotiations with one suitor after another, keeping everyone in suspense, may have seemed to Elizabeth so advantageous that she delayed making a commitment until her time was up and she could no longer have a child. She may have had an unconscious dread of marriage. The fact that her father had had her mother beheaded might well have put family life in a negative light. . . .
>
> As the "Virgin Queen," then, Elizabeth reigned for forty-five years as a quite original phenomenon, married, as she said, to her people, and perhaps feeling at some level that the limitations of mortality did not apply to her and that she need not concern herself with dynastic worries.

Jo McMurtry, *Understanding Shakespeare's England: A Companion for the American Reader.* Hamden, CT: Archon, 1989, p. 31.

The Royal Progresses

Beyond the Privy Council, Elizabeth maintained a large court: a group of aristocrats, both men and women—lords, ladies, knights, dukes, earls, and so on. These aristocrats attended the many functions of state and were always on hand to offer opinions, ideas, and counsel. Over the course of her reign, as many as twelve hundred aristocrats were summoned whenever Elizabeth held court.

The events that members of the court were expected to attend included the innumerable galas staged at the queen's palaces—of which there were five. These events could range from extraordinarily staged costume balls to much quainter evenings of backgammon with close friends. Although the queen loved festive occasions—she fancied herself an excellent dancer and owned more than two thousand ball gowns—these events were staged for more than just entertainment value. The parties, large or small, gave Elizabeth an opportunity to interact with aristocrats who were not members of the Privy Council and to hear ideas on the affairs of state from friends and allies who were not normally close at hand in the palace.

Whenever the queen traveled into the English countryside to visit the many small towns in the realm—which she did very often—members of the court were expected to accompany her. During the Elizabethan era, these trips were known as royal progresses. They usually occurred in the summertime, when Elizabeth found the steamy London weather unbearable. And so she ventured into the English countryside, seeking cool breezes as well as opportunities to greet her subjects. The poor and unwashed farmers and their families lined the muddy and dung-filled English country roads to capture a glimpse of their queen, who enjoyed their adulation immensely. She rode on horseback or in an ornate open carriage, waving to her subjects as they cheered wildly.

WORDS IN CONTEXT

progresses

Travels made by Elizabeth into the English countryside.

For a poor and destitute farmer and his family, the queen's tour of the countryside could seem like a fairy tale come true. The queen always wore a beautiful gown and exquisite jewels. It was very likely the only time in their lives these people witnessed such finery; in their eyes Elizabeth may have appeared more like a goddess than a queen. Moreover, the entourage

This illustration depicts Queen Elizabeth I escorted by courtiers on one of her progresses, journeys made from London into the English countryside to visit rural areas.

of servants and soldiers who accompanied her added to the luster and the grand spectacle that unfolded before the eyes of the people. More than a century after her death, the English poet Alexander Pope translated the ancient Greek poem *The Odyssey*. Historians believe Pope's translation of this verse was inspired by stories he was told of the royal progresses of Elizabeth:

When through the street she gracious deigns to move,
(The public wonder, and the public love,)
The tongues of all with transport sound her praise,
The eyes of all, as on a goddess, gaze.[11]

When the queen arrived in the village of her destination, entertainment was usually provided. A stage, erected beforehand, provided a venue for performances by musicians. Food and drink were served. At night, the villagers could expect a grand display of fireworks. As for the local thieves, prostitutes, beggars, mentally ill persons, and other undesirables, they were rounded up and tossed in the local jailhouse—to be kept far from her majesty's presence for the duration of the queen's visit.

A Dismal Duty

During her visits to the countryside, Elizabeth was accompanied by members of the court. They rode behind the queen's carriage: silent, impassive, and indifferent to the commoners alongside the road. It was a duty abhorred by most members of the court, inasmuch as the country inns the nobles were forced to endure were hardly as comfortable, or the meals as succulent, as what they could expect at their own estates or London mansions. Wrote one anonymous historian of the era, "Nothing save war was more disruptive to the orderly well-being of court life than a Royal progress."[12]

And if a member of the nobility was asked to provide lodging in his country estate home for the queen, it was very likely that he would have to spend large sums of money to prepare the house for the royal visit. Representatives of the queen arrived a week beforehand, bearing trunks of her clothes as well as furnishings to ensure her majesty's comfort during her stay at the residence. Food had to be stockpiled to supply meals to the queen and her attendants. Entertainment had to be provided: Elizabeth enjoyed going for long walks on the estates of her friends. And so they took great pains to spruce up their properties—planting gardens, pulling weeds, cutting trails—all designed so the queen could enjoy a leisurely stroll amid the luxury to which she was accustomed. Elizabeth was adventurous as well and enjoyed hunting deer and small game, and so hunting parties had to be organized. And then, after all that expense, trouble, and toil, after three weeks or so the queen departed and headed home to London.

But members of the court tolerated such distressful missions because there was value in court membership. Foreign ambassadors, men of business or law, or anybody who required the ear of the queen could gain access to her majesty by bribing influential members of the court. To be invited into Elizabeth's court meant evenings filled with parties, the occasional unpleasantness of a trip into the countryside, but also pockets filled with bribes. Wrote nineteenth-century historian Anna Jameson:

> With regard to the state of morals and manners in Elizabeth's court, the first were not better, and the latter not worse, than in other courts of that time. The system of corruption was open and gross, for not only favor, but justice, was to be bought and sold. When we read that Lord [Francis] Bacon was disgraced in the following reign for accepting, or allowing his servants to accept, of bribes in his office, we are at first filled with pity, surprise, and even consternation, that a man so wise and so great, to whom God gave a spirit to comprehend the universe, who was the Columbus of modern philosophy,—that he should thus so poorly degrade himself; but we find that in the court in which he was educated and passed his early probation as a statesman it was a common and general practice.[13]

The Idle Parliament

If the court was a place of merriment, the Parliament was a place of apathy and idleness. During her reign Elizabeth paid Parliament little heed. In truth, Parliament rarely convened during Elizabeth's reign, and when it did she held the power of veto and used it often. Elizabeth believed strongly in the powers of the monarch, and so did many of her subjects.

During the reign of her younger half brother, Edward VI, a book of homilies was published and distributed to all Church of England ministers, who were expected to read its messages to their flocks. The book declared that the monarch was to be regarded as the supreme authority figure of the realm: "It is intolerable ignorance, madness and wickedness for subjects to make any murmuring, rebellion of insurrection against their most dear and most dread sovereign Lord and King, ordained and appointed by God's goodness for their commodity, peace and quietness."[14]

In other words, ministers admonished their church members each Sunday that the queen had been selected by God to rule over the people of England. As for Elizabeth, in a 1566 speech to Parliament she dismissed the authority of England's popularly elected lawmakers with these words: "My Lords, do whatever you wish. As for me, I shall do no otherwise than pleases me."[15]

Death of the Queen

Elizabeth died in 1603 at age sixty-nine. Given the lack of modern medical care in addition to unsanitary conditions and poor nutrition available to the citizens of England during her reign, Elizabeth lived a long life. Even the wealthiest and most aristocratic citizens rarely lived into their sixties. She was succeeded by James I, the son of her cousin Mary Stuart, Queen of Scots—a circumstance she brought upon herself, given her refusal to marry and produce her own heir. Still, in the final years of her life she began a correspondence with James, the king of Scotland, opening up diplomatic channels. She died having never met her successor.

Nearly forty-five years earlier, she had entered the city of London in triumph, leading a parade as her subjects welcomed her with loud cheers. And now, the body of the beloved queen left London in a casket as a slow procession made its way through the glum city streets. Witnessing the scene, the English historian William Camden wrote, "There was such a general sighing and groaning, and weeping, as the like has not been seen or known in the memory of man; neither doth any history mention any people, time or state, to make lamentation for the death of their sovereign."[16]

Chapter Two

Language and Learning in Shakespeare's Day

By the 1580s the mathematician John Dee (who also dabbled in alchemy and astrology) amassed a personal library of some four thousand volumes—believed to be the largest collection of books in England. Throughout his lifetime Dee constantly sought to expand his library—so much so that when he died in 1609 he was virtually penniless, having spent most of his fortune on books.

Dee's library was so popular—it included books published in twenty-one different languages—that scholars from throughout England made their way to his home in the town of Mortlake, just outside London, to consult books in his collection. Describing his library in 1599, Dee wrote, "In this Library, there were about 4000 books, of which 700 were anciently written by hand: some in Greek, some in Latin, some in Hebrew and some in other languages."[17]

> **WORDS IN CONTEXT**
> **alchemy**
> Phony science in which chemicals were applied to ordinary metals, such as lead, with the goal of turning them into gold or silver.

Dee felt beholden to create such a massive library because books were scarce in the England of William Shakespeare. This scarcity dated back to Henry VIII's dispute with the Catholic Church. When Henry stripped the Catholic churches of their property, a lot of their treasures could be found in their libraries. Most churches of the era housed impressive storehouses of books and manuscripts. Starting in 1534, when Henry created the Church of England, vandals were permitted to ransack the Catholic libraries—even the libraries at prominent universities such as Oxford were victimized. One visitor to Oxford wrote of seeing books and manuscripts piled high on the school's campus, where they were offered to local farmers to be shredded for use as stuffing for scarecrows.

A Developing Language

When Elizabeth ascended to the throne in 1558, attitudes toward literature had changed. Indeed, the development of the printing press had a lot to do with the growth in popularity of books in England. Invented in the prior century by the German Johannes Gutenberg, a press featuring moveable type revolutionized printing in Europe and made books widely available. Prior to Gutenberg's breakthrough, most books were reproduced by hand—largely by monks whose orders were devoted to copying, word for word, the few books published in the era.

The printing press arrived in England in 1476 in a London print shop established by William Caxton, who spent four years in the German city of Cologne learning the printing trade. By the 1580s about two dozen print shops could be found in London, with additional printers doing business in other English cities. It was a busy trade. Printers churned out religious tracts, reproductions of Greek and Roman literature, textbooks, and cookbooks. But although books were finding their way into the homes of Londoners and other English citizens, a significant problem remained. By Shakespeare's day, English was still a language in development. Spelling, usage, grammar, punctuation, and all the other elements that make up a language differed from city to city and region to region. In fact, during the Elizabethan era the English alphabet consisted of twenty-four letters—*u* and *v* were used interchangeably, as were *i* and *j*. The *j* was usually substituted for the capital *I* when used to begin a word or sentence; as for the *u*, it was employed in the middle of the word, whereas the *v* was used at the beginning of the word. Moreover, *y* was often used to represent the sound made by *th*. And numbers were often represented by lowercase Roman numerals—except the *j* was substituted for the final *i* in the number. The date May 9, for example, was written "viiij May."

If it all sounds very confusing, well, it was. Caxton himself was among the first to call attention to the need to standardize the English

William Caxton, depicted in this illustration, was the owner of the first printing press in England. Caxton championed standardizing the English language, which varied widely from region to region.

language when he commented on the plight of an unfortunate sailor on a mission to buy meat (mete) and eggs (eggys or egges). The sailor's English (englysshe) was so poor that a housewife (good wyf) mistook his speech for French (frenshe):

> That comyn englysshe that is spoken in one shyre varyeth from another. . . . [A sailor] named sheffelde a mercer came in to an hows and axed for mete and specyally he axyd after eggys And

the goode wyf answerde that she coude speke no frenshe. And the marchaut was angry for he also coude speke no frenshe. but wolde haue hadde egges and she vnderstode hym not And thenne at laste a nother sayd that he wolde haue eyren then the good wyf sayd that she vnderstod hym well Loo what sholde a man in thyse dayes now wryte. egges or eyren certynly it is harde to playse euery man by cause of dyuersitie & chauge of langage.[18]

The First Dictionary

An early attempt to standardize the English language occurred during Shakespeare's lifetime. In 1604 schoolmaster Robert Cawdrey published what is regarded as the first English dictionary, which he titled *A Table Alphabeticall*. It was a modest effort, to be sure, including fewer than three thousand words, for which Cawdrey provided only the briefest of definitions. Moreover, Cawdrey did not even define or attempt to spell words that were in common use; rather, he limited the dictionary to "hard words," which he defined as words new to the English language. These consisted mainly of terms from French, Latin, and other languages that were finding their way into daily use by English speakers.

Explaining the purpose of his dictionary, Cawdrey wrote in the introduction:

> A Table Alphabetical, conteyning and teaching the true writing, and understanding of hard usuall English wordes, borrowed from the Hebrew, Greeke, Latine, or French &c. With the interpretation thereof by plaine English words, gathered for the benefit & helpe of Ladies, Gentlewomen, or any other unskillfull persons. Whereby they may the more easilie and better understand many hard English wordes, which they shall heare or read in Scriptures, Sermons, or elsewhere, and also be made able to use the same aptly themselves.[19]

Certainly, any modern student of English would blanch at Cawdrey's own spelling and usage issues. Admonishing users of his dictionary to first learn the alphabet, Cawdrey wrote: "If thou be desirous (gentle Reader) rightly and readily to vnderstand, and to profit by this Table. . . . Then thou must learne the Alphabet, to wit, the order of letters as they stand, perfectly without booke, and where euery Letter standeth, as (b) neere the beginning, (n) about the middest, and (t) toward the end."[20]

Illiteracy in Elizabethan England

As Cawdrey's own writing illustrates, spelling was done by guesswork—even Shakespeare was not sure how to spell his own name. Historians have found signatures by the playwright using these variations: Willm Shaksp, William Shakespe, Wm Shakspe, William Shakspere, Willm Shakspere, and William Shakspeare. The spelling most commonly used today, William Shakespeare, is drawn from dedications of two of his poems, "Venus and Adonis" and "Lucrece," to his patron, the earl of Lancaster. (Patrons provided financial backing to the artists and writers of the era.) In the dedications, Shakespeare uses the spelling found commonly today. Since correspondence between writers and their patrons was of the utmost importance, historians believe Shakespeare took pains to get the spelling right. And so the name "William Shakespeare" has been accepted as proper and can be found on his works that have been published over the past four centuries.

If stumbling over a wide variety of spellings did not make reading hard enough, lovers of literature in Elizabethan England were plagued by another sad fact of the era: By the time Shakespeare started writing plays and sonnets, about half of the population of England could not read. Formal education was denied to all but those with the means to afford it.

Indeed, by the early years of the sixteenth century even many aristocrats did not see the importance of formal educations for their children: Sons of the landed gentry were taught to ride and hunt and not much else. In 1531, though, the philosopher Thomas Elyot published the influential essay *The Governour* in which he emphasized the importance of education for the ruling classes, and soon the sons of aristocrats and eventually others found themselves sitting in classrooms. In 1601, the Elizabethan era English philosopher Francis Bacon wrote that for aristocrats to take their rightful places as leaders of government, business, and law, they must attend school and be well-read and well-educated. He said, "For expert men can execute, and perhaps judge of particulars, one by one; but that general counsels, and the plots of marshalling of affairs, come best from those that are learned."[21]

Petty Schools

By the end of the 1500s, the children of aristocrats learned at home, educated by private tutors hired by their parents. Most other children whose parents could afford to provide them with formal educations attended "petty schools"—classes held in the homes of teachers who were paid directly by parents. The term probably comes from the French word *petite*, meaning "tiny." In most cases the teachers were usually educated housewives, who may have advanced beyond petty school education themselves. (Another name for the petty school was the dame school.) Petty school students were taught to read and write. They also received lessons in the Bible as well as lessons in behavior.

WORDS IN CONTEXT

petty school

The first school attended by most English children, usually until they reached age seven. For many girls petty school was likely to be their only formal schooling.

This twentieth-century print shows Shakespeare and his theatrical troupe performing for Queen Elizabeth I and her court.

Shakespeare, the son of a glove maker who was by no means wealthy, attended a petty school in the town of his birth—Stratford-upon-Avon, a village on the Avon River about 78 miles (126 km) northwest of London. Looking back on his school days, Shakespeare wrote:

The whining schoolboy, with his satchel
And shining morning face, creeping like snail
Unwilling to school.[22]

Each petty school student received a hornbook, which was actually a wooden paddle on which a sheet of parchment had been pasted. Inscribed on the parchment was the English alphabet and usually a religious prayer.

Educating Girls

At age seven most boys left the petty schools to attend grammar schools. Often sponsored by the local trade or craft guilds, grammar school teachers were known as ushers. In most cases ushers were senior students at the grammar schools. At grammar school, students were often introduced to their first textbook—a volume on Latin written by William Lily, whose textbook had been authorized by Henry VIII as the sole source of Latin education for all English schoolchildren.

One element of a student's education that was invariably neglected was handwriting. Ushers believed penmanship was of little importance and instead left the task to an educator known as a scrivener. Scriveners traveled from school to school, spending just a few weeks a year at each school teaching students how to form letters with their quill pens and inkwells.

When students reached age ten, masters took over their grammar school classrooms. The masters were professional teachers. Under their guidance boys learned Latin and Greek, reading dramas written by the ancient Roman and Greek playwrights. Religious education was still emphasized. Also, at this age boys were introduced to their first lessons in arithmetic.

Girls also attended petty schools—if their parents could afford the tuition. Few girls continued to grammar schools; instead, young girls of grammar school age were expected to stay home to help their mothers with the housework. Daughters of aristocrats were tutored at home, where they learned to speak Latin, Greek, and French. They were taught music and dancing—very important skills for a future lady of the aristocracy—as well as manners and etiquette. Some of these girls were sent to live in the homes of other aristocrats, where they learned how to run a large household. The supervision of servants and maintenance of wardrobes were important skills high-born young women were expected to learn. As they grew older, girls were never sent to the universities of the era. Invariably, by their early teen years, they were married off to the sons of nobles. In the sixteenth century it was legal for a girl to marry as early as age twelve. Moreover, it was the rare occasion when the marriage of an aristocrat's daughter was not arranged by the two families.

> **WORDS IN CONTEXT**
> **usher**
> A teacher in a grammar school, often a senior student.

Completely left out of formal education were the children of the poor or even those of some means who could not afford petty school or grammar school tuition or whose parents simply preferred not to send them to school. Farm boys were needed at home to help their fathers with the many chores of agricultural work. Girls were needed to help their mothers with the housework as well as whatever other chores they could do around the farm, such as tending gardens or milking cows. All work on the farm was performed with manual labor; therefore, farmers valued whatever labor they could find—even the labor of their young children.

Discipline by the Switch

By age fourteen the boys of the working classes left grammar school to begin apprenticeships in the trades or crafts, while boys of high birth could expect to be boarded at such schools as Eton or Winchester. For the children of the privileged, the school day was very long—starting at five o'clock in the morning, when they were roused out of their beds,

In Their Own Words

Should Girls Be Educated?

Girls received little formal education during William Shakespeare's lifetime. Even so, there were many advocates for providing girls with as much formal education as boys. One strong advocate for providing girls with more schooling was Richard Mulcaster, a member of Parliament who advocated more education for all English citizens. In 1581 Mulcaster wrote that girls should learn to read and write and also receive training in music and mathematics. He wrote:

> Where the question is how much a woman ought to learn, the answer may be, so much as be needful. . . . This *how much* consisteth either in perfecting . . . reading well, writing fair, singing sweet, playing fine, beyond all cry and above all comparison, that pure excellency in these things but ordinary may cause extraordinary liking; or else in skill of languages annexed to these four, that more good gifts may work wonder. . . . I fear no workmanship in women to give them geometry and her sister sciences, to make them mathematicals.

Quoted in R.E. Pritchard, *Shakespeare's England: Life in Elizabethan and Jacobean Times.* Gloucestershire, England: Sutton, 1999, p. 94.

and lasting through five or six o'clock in the evening. Breaks of fifteen or thirty minutes were granted to the students throughout the day. Classes were in session six days a week; Sundays were devoted to churchgoing.

The typical school of the era featured a huge central hall with rows of benches and desks. All classes were taught in the central hall simultaneously,

A teacher administers physical punishment to an errant student. Discipline was strictly maintained in English schools during Shakespeare's time, and it was common for students who broke the rules to be dealt with harshly.

with students grouped together before their teachers. Discipline was maintained with a switch cut from a birch tree. Richard Mulcaster, a member of Parliament who believed very strongly in education, endorsed the switch as the one true method of keeping order in the classroom. Said Mulcaster, "If that instrument be thought too severe for boys, which was not devised by our time, but received from antiquity, I will not strive with any man in its defence if he will leave us some means for compelling obedience where numbers have to be taught together."[23]

To avoid the switch, boys knew they had to study hard—a wrong answer could be rewarded with several cracks across the rump. In 1639 an aristocrat, R. Willis, wrote a book about his childhood and school days, describing the rigors of his schoolwork. In his account Willis explained that tutors known as "prompters" were often on hand to provide assistance in the classroom—helping students answer questions posed by the teacher. In this case, though, the teacher—angry at Willis (for a reason Willis does not explain)—told Willis he had to answer the questions about vocabulary without help from his prompter. Willis was certain that a wrong answer would lead to a painful experience. He explained:

> **WORDS IN CONTEXT**
> **switch**
> A small branch cut from a birch tree; used for discipline in the classroom.

In his anger, to do me the greatest hurt he could (which then he thought to be, to fall under the rod) he dealt with all the prompters, that none of them should help me, and so (as he thought) I must necessarily be beaten. When I found myself at this strait, I gathered all my wits together (as we say) and listened the more carefully to my fellows that instruct before me, and having also some easy word to my lot for parsing I made hard shrift escape for that time. And when I observed my adversary's displeasure to continue against me, so as I could have no help from my prompters, I doubled my diligence and attention to our master's construing our next lesson to us, and observing carefully how in construction one word followed and depended upon another, which heedful observing two or three lessons more, opened the way to . . . me . . . so as I needed no prompter.[24]

University Life

After reaching age fourteen, the sons of aristocrats were expected to enroll in universities at Oxford or Cambridge—colleges that were already well established by Shakespeare's day. Subjects taught at the universities included philosophy, rhetoric, poetry, natural history, grammar, logic,

Looking Back

Learning to Be a Clergyman

Joining the ranks of the clergy in Elizabethan England was, perhaps, the most difficult of all career paths. After spending eight years at either Oxford or Cambridge, prospective clergymen were expected to study for another ten years at divinity schools before they were accepted into the Church of England clergy. Says English historian Ian Mortimer:

> If you decide to do a third degree [after master of arts], you can choose between a doctorate in civil law or medicine, or continue to study divinity. The last is the hardest option: you must study for a minimum of seven years after receiving your master of arts degree; the actual doctorate then takes another three years. The whole process of becoming a doctor of divinity thus lasts at least eighteen years—so think carefully before embarking on this career path. Given the high mortality in towns, there is a 40 percent chance you will die before you graduate.

Ian Mortimer, *The Time Traveler's Guide to Elizabethan England.* New York: Viking, 2012, p. 89.

music, astronomy, mathematics, and religion. Students spent as long as eight years in their university studies. After four years, they were awarded a bachelor of arts degree; after eight years, a master of arts degree.

The work was not easy: Students could expect to spend long hours in study—although they were helped by tutors who visited their rooms at night to read to them. Explaining the life of a university student, Church of England bishop John Earle wrote, "He has a strange forced appetite to learning, and to achieve it brings nothing but patience and a body. His study is not great but continual, and consists much in the sitting up after midnight in a rug gown and a nightcap, to the vanquishing perhaps of some six lines; yet what he has, he has perfect, for he reads it so long to understand it till he gets it without book."[25]

For most students, university life consisted of more than endless studying: Students also took lessons in dancing, tennis, and fencing. Recreation could be found in the off-campus taverns, where university students flocked for relaxation.

The Grand Tour

Following graduation, and before joining the world of the aristocracy and all it demanded, a young man of means was given the gift of the grand tour. The tradition, which started during the Elizabethan years, involved young university graduates taking leisurely journeys across the continent of Europe—sometimes for as long as two or three years. During their travels, these young men were expected to study the art, languages, and literature of the great European cities. The poet Philip Sidney, whose own journey began in 1572, is believed to have been the first grand tourist. Sidney visited Paris and Strasbourg in France; Frankfurt and Heidelberg in Germany; Vienna, Austria; and Venice, Italy. Upon his return, Elizabeth granted a knighthood to Sidney and selected him for a diplomatic post. Counseling other young men about to embark of their grand tours, Francis Bacon wrote:

The things to be seen and observed are: the courts of princes, specially when they give audience to ambassadors; the courts of justice, where they sit and hear causes, and so of consistories ecclesiastic; the churches and monasteries, with the monuments which are therein extant; the walls and fortifications of cities and towns, and so the havens and harbours; antiquities and ruins; libraries; colleges; disputations and lectures, where any are; shipping and navies; houses and gardens of state and pleasure, near great cities; armouries; arsenals; magazines [ammunition depots]; exchanges;

burses [stock exchanges]; warehouses; exercises of horsemanship, fencing, training of soldiers, and the like; comedies, whereunto the better sort of persons do resort; treasures of jewels and robes; cabinets and rarities; and, to conclude, whatsoever is memorable in the places where they go.[26]

Pleasures of Their Wealth

Their grand tours concluded, the young men of the aristocracy returned to England. Some enrolled in law schools or medical schools or entered the clergy of the Church of England. Others joined their family businesses, helped run their family estates, entered politics, and perhaps even joined the court of Elizabeth. The young men of the aristocracy, and the daughters of the aristocrats they married, were now prepared for a lifetime of enjoying the pleasures of their wealth. After finishing their formal educations they were expected to take their places in a society that was mostly closed to the members of the poorly educated masses of England who lived in the stiflingly crowded cities or muddy farms and villages.

Chapter Three

City Life and Country Life

In William Shakespeare's lifetime, England was predominantly a rural country—most people lived on farms or in the eight hundred tiny villages that dotted the countryside. There were a handful of small cities—Norwich, Bristol, Newcastle, and York, among others. Populations in those cities ranged from ten thousand to thirty thousand. London, however, was a far different city. In 1600 its population stood at two hundred thousand—in Europe, only Paris and Naples were larger. London was the cultural center of England, the seat of English government and law, and the center of virtually all British commerce.

In 1606 the poet Thomas Dekker described life in London:

In every street, carts and coaches make such a thundering as if the world ran upon wheels; at every corner, men, women and children meet in such shoals [atop sand banks], that posts are set up of purpose to strengthen the houses, lest jostling one another they should shoulder them down. Besides, hammers are beating in one place, tubs hooping [a process for wrapping metal bands around wooden pails] in another, pots clinking in a third, water-tankards [water carts] running at tilt in a fourth. Here are porters sweating under burdens, there merchants' men bearing bags of money. Chapmen [street vendors] as if they were at leap-frog skip out of one shop into another. Tradesmen (as if they are danc[ers]) are lusty at legs and never stand still.[27]

London was also a city of contrasts. The eastern half of the city was a busy district covering about a square mile (2.6 sq km), bounded on the south by the Thames River and surrounded on three sides by an ancient Roman wall. It was crowded with townhouses, apartments, rooming houses, inns, workhouses, shops, marketplaces, and textile factories. The streets bustled with people and horses while dogs ran underfoot and farmers herded pigs and other livestock to the markets. Pedestrians had to be just as wary of stepping in animal dung as avoiding pickpockets. To the west, a single road known as the Strand connected the district of Westminster to the rest of London.

> **WORDS IN CONTEXT**
> **chapmen**
> Street vendors.

Westminster was a place of wealth. Every morning, lawyers and other wealthy Westminster residents strolled leisurely along the mansion-lined Strand to their offices in London. Westminster enjoyed cleaner air and cleaner streets than could be found in the city. Additionally, most of Westminster's estates fronted the river. This allowed wealthy Londoners to travel in their own barges and avoid the dangerous rural roads where robbers were known to lurk.

The Inns of London

To enter London, a visitor passed through one of many gatehouses built into the ancient Roman walls. Toll takers manned the gatehouses, meaning visitors had to pay tolls to enter. They also had to be prepared to answer questions about their business in the city—undesirables were not wanted in London. Indeed, each tollhouse included a small jail where suspected thieves, beggars, and other criminals were confined if they were caught trying to sneak into the city.

In the city a visitor's first mission was finding lodgings. If friends or family members were not providing a bed for the night, the visitor made his or her way to one of the many inns doing business in the city. Most of the inns were so-called inn-yards: three-story structures erected in a square and featuring a central yard. Balconies for the inside rooms looked over the yard. The larger inns employed musicians and singers to

In Their Own Words

London Bridge

Erected in the twelfth century, by William Shakespeare's day London Bridge was one of the busiest thoroughfares in London. Spanning the Thames River, London Bridge was lined with homes and shops, making it appear as an ordinary street rather than a bridge. The original London Bridge was destroyed in the Great Fire of London in 1666. Describing the bridge in 1617, the aristocrat and author Fynes Moryson wrote:

The bridge at London is worthily to be numbered among the miracles of the world, if men respect the building and foundation laid artificially and stately over an ebbing and flowing water upon 21 piles of stone, with 20 arches, under which barks [three-masted ships] pass, the lowest foundation being (as they say) packs of wool, most durable against the force of water, and not to be repaired but upon great fall of the waters and by artificial turning or stopping the course of them; or if men expect the houses upon the bridge, as great and high as those of the firm land, so as a man cannot know that he passeth a bridge, but would judge himself to be in the street, say that the houses on both sides are combined in the top, making the passage somewhat dark, and that in some few open places the river of Thames may be seen on both sides.

Quoted in R.E. Pritchard, *Shakespeare's England: Life in Elizabethan and Jacobean Times.* Gloucestershire, England: Sutton, 1999, p. 154.

entertain guests in the yard. Inns featured stables for the travelers' horses. And of course, each inn featured a tavern.

In 1587 the Church of England clergyman William Harrison boasted that English inns were the finest in all of Europe. Wrote Harrison:

> In all our inns we have plenty of ale, beer, and sundry kinds of wine, and such is the capacity of some of them that they are able to lodge two hundred or three hundred persons and their horses at ease, and thereto with a very short warning make such provisions for their diet as to him that is unacquainted withal may seem to be incredible. Howbeit, of all in England there are no worse inns than in London, and yet many are there far better than the best that I have heard of in any foreign country, if all circumstances be duly considered.[28]

Inns line the entrance to London in this 1909 illustration depicting Elizabethan England. These establishments provided lodging for the many visitors to the capital.

Seasoned travelers who visited the London inns knew to be wary, though. It was not unusual for an innkeeper to be in cahoots with a high-wayman. Upon learning of the traveler's plans, the crooked innkeeper passed the information on to his ally, who laid a trap for the hapless traveler well beyond the city limits. The innkeeper, Harrison warned, "thereof giveth warning to such odd guests as haunt the house and are of his confederacy, to the utter undoing of many an honest yeoman as he journeyeth by the way."[29]

Marketplaces and Factories

Once lodgings had been secured, travelers made their way onto the streets to pursue whatever business brought them to the city. Exploring London streets, visitors found marketplaces where vendors set up stalls to sell meat, fish, poultry, milk, eggs, vegetables, fruits, and baked goods. Other vendors were simply women carrying baskets of cherries, plums, or other fruits. "Oranges and lemons!"[30] was a common cry heard in the aisles of a London marketplace.

Butchers also plied their trade in the London marketplaces. Farmers herded their cows, sheep, and pigs to the butcher's stand. Chickens were carried in cages. For shoppers who desired a quick meal, marketplace vendors sold pasties. These were made of meats cooked into small pies—a sort of fast food of the era. Pasties were washed down with ale—also available from many marketplace vendors.

All manner of trade and craft shops lined the city streets. Many Londoners worked as tailors, shoemakers, barbers, candle makers, gold-smiths, printers, clock makers, carpenters, and masons. Organizations known as "companies" oversaw employment in most of the trades. To find work as a carpenter, for example, a Londoner had to join the Wor-shipful Company of Carpenters.

Workers in the trades and crafts were expected to labor for long hours—usually from dawn until after dusk. Pay was low and the work often backbreaking. Some employees were lucky enough to be provided meals by their bosses. Often, the fruits, vegetables, and meats given to the workers were procured at the London marketplaces just a day or so before the vendors were likely to have tossed them due to rot.

Elizabethan London was a thriving business center that was home to numerous street vendors, along with trade and craft shops like the cobbler shop depicted here.

Amid the craftsmen and street vendors, a visitor to the London of the late 1500s could also find the first evidence of industrialization. More than a century before the invention of the steam engine in 1712 led to the widespread industrialization of Europe, some enterprising merchants in the fabric trade saw the value in mass production. A handful of fabric factories were established in the London of Shakespeare's day—some employing as many as two hundred women to weave fabric at hand-operated looms. Women also worked as wool carders—using their fingers or rudimentary tools to pick the knots out of wool, preparing it to be spun into thread.

Still, many Londoners lacked employment—during Shakespeare's lifetime, the population of London grew faster than the city's economy could accommodate. Moreover, unemployment was regarded harshly by the authorities. People without jobs could be jailed while the authorities searched for work for them to do. Girls over age twelve and women under age forty could be forced to perform menial chores for whomever the authorities found to employ them. For unemployed able-bodied men—according to English law, that included boys over age twelve and men under age sixty—the English government held the power to send them into the countryside to work on farms.

"Evil Stink" of the City

One area where employment was often in demand was in the care and husbandry of horses. In the centuries before mechanization, horses performed most of the heavy labor—hauling goods in wagons, pulling plows, or toting carriages filled with riders. Thousands of Londoners worked in stables or as saddle makers, blacksmiths, wheelwrights, and similar occupations.

Of course, with horses and other animals so common in the streets, sanitation was virtually nonexistent. As a result, the city was rife with noxious odors—a circumstance that led the well-to-do and others who could afford it to carry herbs and flowers with them, which they held under their noses when the odors became unbearable. Many people looked forward to the spring mornings, when the breezes of the season carried the much more pleasing aromas of the wildflower fields outside the city into the London streets.

Bathing was also not an everyday occurrence in a London home. Indoor plumbing was still centuries in the future—people used chamber pots, also known as jakes, typically emptying them in the streets and alleys or directly into the Thames. The sixteenth-century physician Simon Forman described the conditions of his lodging house, where he saw his patients. "The evil stink of the privy did annoy me much and because many [clients] did resort unto me there I left it because it was little and too high up and because of the stink."[31] Moreover, rainwater washed the human and animal feces into the Thames, which is where many Londoners filled jugs with water to take home for drinking and bathing.

WORDS IN CONTEXT
jake
A common name for the chamber pot, used in the years before indoor plumbing and flush toilets became common in households.

In 1596 Sir John Harrington, godson of the queen, invented what could have helped London rid itself of the all-too-pervasive stink when he fashioned what is believed to have been history's first flush toilet. He made two—one for himself, the other for his godmother—and even published a book describing his invention, *The Metamorphosis of Ajax*. ("Ajax" is the name given to the device by Harrington, a variation on the word *jake*. Today the word *john* is often substituted for the word *toilet*, so-named in honor of its inventor.) But critics thought the device folly and mocked Harrington. He never built another toilet—and for many centuries London remained an unsanitary and squalid city of chamber pots and foulsmelling streets.

Disease and Fire

The lax sanitation of the city led to the spread of diseases. Medical science was in its infancy, and it would be centuries before physicians linked germs with the spread of disease. Typhoid, smallpox, influenza, and tuberculosis were ever-present threats to Londoners. Even more serious was the threat of bubonic plague. Occasional outbreaks during the Elizabethan era took the lives of ten thousand or more Londoners. During one outbreak of the plague in 1603, Dekker described a dismal scene: streets

Looking Back

The Country Gentlemen

Farmers did all the work on their farms, but few of them actually owned their land. During the lifetime of William Shakespeare, most of the agricultural land was located on the country estates of aristocrats who lived in London. A few country squires did reside on their rural estates, but those cases were rare. Wealthy people preferred to live in London, where they could mingle among their own kind, join the queen's court, and attend the many galas reserved for their class. Left on the land were the farmers, who saw little profit from their toil. Says Jo McMurtry, professor of English at the University of Richmond in Virginia:

> The traditional country squire rebelled against his tradition, got tired of living in the country, bought a house in London, and spent most of his time there.
>
> The absentee landlord was seen by many observers in the sixteenth century as a major cause of rural troubles. Instead of belonging to the land and seeing it and its human inhabitants as an organic unity, the absentee was envisioned sitting in London and crunching numbers, as we might put it—concerned only with the profit land would bring him.

Jo McMurtry, *Understanding Shakespeare's England: A Companion for the American Reader.* Hamden, CT: Archon, 1989, p. 103.

deserted at night, mournful wails emanating from homes, death ever present in the neighborhoods:

> Would not the strongest-hearted man, beset with such a ghastly horror, look wild, and run mad, and die? And even such a formidable shape did the diseased City appear in: for he that durst [dared], in the dead hour of gloomy midnight, have been so valiant as to have walked through the still and melancholy streets, what think you should have been his music? Surely the loud groans of raving, sick men; the struggling pangs of souls departing; in every house grief striking up an alarum; servants crying out for masters, wives for husbands, parents for children, children for their mother.[32]

The worst was yet to come. Not too far in the future—in 1665—the Great Plague took the lives of some one hundred thousand Londoners.

Fire was also a threat. Buildings were made of wood, lighting was provided through candles, cooking was done over an open fire, and heating was fueled by wood as well. A stray spark could be disastrous, and in fact, fires were common. Just a year after the Great Plague, London was hit by the Great Fire, which destroyed huge tracts of the city.

Fun in Old London

Disease, stench, deadly fires, backbreaking labor, rotting food—the London of Shakespeare's time did have its downsides. But there was enormous fun to be had if one knew where to find it. Cockfights were a popular pastime for those with money to gamble. Tennis was a particularly popular sport among aristocrats. The sport of rowing may have had its roots in the Elizabethan era as young men raced boats on the Thames, using barrel staves—the thin curved planks that form barrel walls—as oars. By Shakespeare's day, jousting—in which two knights in armor charged one another on horseback in an attempt to impale one's opponent—had

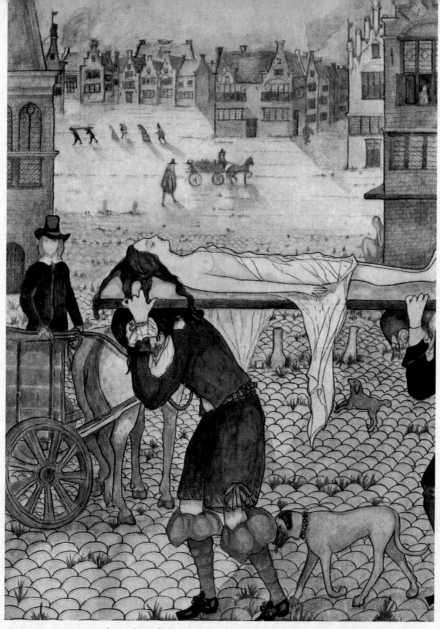

Devastating outbreaks of diseases, including bubonic plague, were a commonplace facet of life in seventeenth-century England. The Great Plague of London in 1665, a scene of which is depicted here, killed an estimated 100,000 people.

long fallen into history, but a form of jousting known as quintain was very popular. In quintain, competitors on horseback charged a target hung to a post. The competitor who stuck his lance closest to the bull's-eye was declared the winner.

Elsewhere in London, young men engaged in competitions in wrestling, shooting, and fencing. The sports of bullbaiting and bearbaiting were also popular. In bullbaiting, a bull was chained to a post. A man leading a dog approached the bull, and for about an hour the chained beast and dog would snap at each other as the man and his dog did their best to avoid the lethal horns of the bull. Elizabeth was a big fan of bullbaiting and often attended competitions held in specially built bullbaiting arenas. A similar sport was bearbaiting, in which young men tested their courage by essentially playing tag with the beasts, which were chained to posts. The object of the sport was to approach the bear with a dog, inching close enough to smack the bear with a tree branch while avoiding the animal's claws and jaws. Robert Laneham, a member of the Privy Council, often accompanied the queen to bearbaiting events. He recalled:

It was a sport very pleasant to see, to see the bear, with his pink eyes, tearing after his enemies approach; the nimbleness . . . of the dog to take his advantage and the force and experience of the bear again to avoid his assaults: if he were bitten in one place how he would pinch in another to get free; that if he were taken once, then by what shift with biting, with clawing, with roaring, with tossing and tumbling he would work and wind himself from them; and when he was loose to shake his ears twice or thrice with the blood and the slaver [saliva] hanging about his physiognomy.[33]

Finally, in the evening, after a busy day at the market or a vigorous day of rowing along the Thames or participating in a quintain joust or attending a bullbaiting contest, a young man might seek the entertainment of a London brothel, of which there were many. Dekker, ashamed that his city was home to so many houses of prostitution, wrote, "The doors of notorious carted bawds like Hell gates stand night and day wide open, with a pair of harlots in taffeta gowns, like two painted posts, garnishing out those doors, being better to the house than a double sign."[34]

The Rural Life

For people who lived in the country, there were no grand rowing contests on the Thames and no quintain competitions. There were also fewer brothels. And so country life lacked many of the pleasures and entertainments one could find in the city. However, many of the discomforts of the city were very much a part of country life. Certainly, things did not smell much better—there was still plenty of dung underfoot. In Shakespeare's comedy *As You Like It*, the aristocrat Touchstone finds himself on a rural English sheep farm. Touchstone declares—right after he steps in a pile of sheep dung—that country life is not for him. "It goes much against my stomach,"[35] he huffs.

In the countryside a farmer's life was one of unending toil, but by Elizabeth's time at least farmers were no longer virtual slaves. For centuries criminals or citizens in debt could be sold as slaves and put to work on farms, but in the medieval era slavery died out in England and was replaced by the system known as serfdom. Serfs were not much better off than slaves. They labored on lands owned by aristocrats and then were forced to pay rent and turn over most of their crops to the landowners. Under law, they were beholden to remain on the land for their entire lives, as were their children and children's children.

> **WORDS IN CONTEXT**
> **quintain**
> A sport with roots in the medieval joust; competitors on horseback aimed their lances at a stationary target.

The end of serfdom in England has its roots in the Peasant's Revolt of 1381—a largely unsuccessful uprising in which serfs marched on London and demanded their freedom. King Richard II reneged on his promise to outlaw serfdom. Nevertheless, the effects of the revolt reverberated throughout England as nervous landowners feared for their safety and, on their own, granted the serfs the freedom they desired. Finally, in 1574 an official edict by Elizabeth outlawed serfdom.

Despite winning their freedom, the former serfs found themselves earning lean profits—a main reason London exploded in population during Elizabeth's reign. During the era many farms were still located on the estates of the aristocrats, who took the major share of the profits from the labors of the farmers. Unable to find much opportunity in the fields, people flocked to London in search of better lives.

The Farmer's Day

A farmer who managed to attain some measure of prosperity might have built his home from bricks or stones. But most farmers lived in timber-framed homes with the seams between the timbers filled with a paste of mud and straw. Roofs were made of straw or reeds, which provided nesting places for rodents and insects. Typically, a farmer's home consisted of two rooms—a kitchen in the front room and single bedroom in the rear where the whole family slept and likely shared the same bed. As in a city home, there was no indoor plumbing, but at least the farm family could make use of an outdoor latrine. Homes were heated by open hearths; many lacked chimneys, which meant the inhabitants had to live under a cloud of smoke.

In the fields farmers raised grains—wheat, rye, oats, and barley. These were the basic ingredients for bread, porridge, and ale. Oats were an important crop since they were fed to horses. Peas, beans, cherries, and apples were also grown on English farms. Many farmers grew crops used in the textile industry. These included flax for linen and hemp for rope and cloth. They also grew flowers such as rose madder and woad; London fabric makers found these useful for making dyes.

Farmers worked long, hard days. Describing the day of a farmer, essayist John Stephens wrote in 1615, "He is an honest man: and so he thinks of no rising higher but rising early morning; and being up, he hath no end of motion, but wanders in his woods and pastures so continually that when he sleeps or sits, he wanders also. After this, he turns into his element, by being too venturous hot and cold: then he is fit for nothing but a chequered grave."[36]

Duties of the Farmwife

The wives of farmers toiled as well. Farmwives were expected to perform all housework and tend to the children. They rose before their husbands to build the fires to cook breakfast. They were responsible for cooking all other meals as well as keeping the homes clean—a burdensome task, given that many farmhouses featured dirt floors, with mice and rats likely to be living in the thatched roofs. Farmwives also made clothes, kept clothes in repair, and did all the laundry in the running waters of a nearby stream.

The life of a farmwife included more than just housework. Farmwives brewed ale, both for their husbands and for sale at the local village marketplace. Farmwives were also expected to perform many duties around the farm, such as milking cows or feeding the chickens and pigs. Other duties included driving the grain to the mill to be ground into flour or making bread and cheese. Many farmwives also tended their own gardens beside the farmhouse, growing herbs and vegetables.

During harvest time, a farmwife might be needed in the fields to help cut and bind the grains. Using scythes and sickles, farmwives chopped hay, then helped rope the hay into bundles and stack it into carts. Although English law and tradition granted all authority in running the farm and the household to the husband, in truth no English farm could survive without the toil of the farmwife. In the 1523 *Book of Husbandry*, one of the first books written about the life of the English farmer, author Sir Anthony Fitzherbert explained:

> WORDS IN CONTEXT
> **scythe and sickle**
> Hand tools for cutting crops; the scythe featured a long handle and long, curved blade; the sickle featured a short handle and small, semicircular blade.

It is a wife's occupation to winnow all manner of corns, to make malt, wash and wring, to make hay, to shear corn, and in time of need to help her husband to fill the . . . dung cart, drive the plough, to load hay, corn and such other. Also to go or ride to the market to sell butter, cheese, milk, eggs, chickens, capons, hens, pigs, geese and all manner of corn. And also to buy all manner of necessary things belonging to a household, and to make true reckoning and account to her husband what hath received and what she hath paid. And if the husband go to the market to buy or sell (as they often do), he then show his wife in like manner. For if one of them should use to deceive the other, he deceiveth himself, and he is not like to thrive, and therefore they must be true either to other.[37]

Center of Commerce

London in the time of Shakespeare was a place of disease, squalor, fire, and endless toil in the cities, while in the countryside, farmers found themselves not much better off than in the era of serfdom. And yet during these hard times, English society flourished. In the cities the merchant class laid the foundation for the Industrial Revolution that arrived a century later, making England into one of the wealthiest countries in Europe. In the countryside the life of a farmer could be filled with backbreaking work; nevertheless, the English farms fed the nation and also provided the raw materials that made England a center of world commerce.

Chapter Four

Crime and Punishment

The Tower of London stands tall on the north bank of the Thames River, a fixture in the city since it was erected by the king William the Conqueror in 1078. The structure was originally constructed as a fortress—its four towers are 90 feet (27 m) tall, with some walls 15 feet (4.6 m) thick. By the era of Henry VIII and his daughter Mary, the Tower served as a prison where hundreds of the monarchs' enemies were tortured and executed.

Under Elizabeth the Tower continued to serve as a prison. Although she had been jailed in the Tower and had faced execution herself, Elizabeth showed no hesitancy about tossing her enemies in the Tower as well. In 1597 a Catholic priest, John Gerard, was charged with plotting against the queen's rule. He was arrested and marched into the Tower, where his torturers demanded he confess. Gerard eventually managed to escape and flee to the European continent, where he wrote about his ordeal in the tower. Recalled Gerard:

> We went to the torture room in a kind of solemn procession, the guards walking ahead with lighted candles. The chamber was underground and dark, particularly near the entrance. It was a vast shadowy place and every device and instrument of human torture was there. They pointed out some of them to me and said that I [w]ould have to taste of them. Then they asked me again if I would confess. "I cannot," I said.[38]

Instruments of Torture

By William Shakespeare's era, torture was a widely employed method for extracting confessions from suspects and meting out punishments to criminals. Elsewhere in Europe torture was used in Spain, Italy, and France during the era of the Holy Inquisition. Starting in the thirteenth century, officers of the Catholic Church, known as inquisitors, used torture to root out heretics—Protestants, Jews, Muslims, and others whom they believed defied the authority of the pope. Their methods found their way to England as well, where monarchs readily employed torture to deal with their enemies.

In 1580 the Catholic priest Edward Rishton was imprisoned in the Tower. Charged with treason, he was sentenced to death. Rishton spent nearly five years in the Tower but in 1584 Queen Elizabeth, with no explanation, commuted his sentence to exile from England. He settled in France. Before his death in 1585, Rishton described the conditions and devices used to torture the prisoners. Dungeons were typically small, he said, with ceilings so low prisoners were unable to stand erect. One place where inmates were held was known as the Pit, a subterranean cave entirely without light.

One device used in the Tower was the rack: A prisoner was laid on the rack, his or her hands and feet tied to rollers that were wound with winches. With each turn of the winch, arms and legs were pulled out of their sockets—an excruciatingly painful punishment.

WORDS IN CONTEXT

scavenger's daughter

A metal hoop placed around a kneeling man or woman; when tightened the torture device applied painful pressure to the shoulders and spine.

Another painful instrument was known as the scavenger's daughter. It was a large metal ring wrapped around a prisoner who was forced to kneel with head down to his or her knees. The ring was then tightened, essentially squeezing the prisoner, exerting painful pressure on the shoulders and spine. Rishton also described iron gauntlets—iron rings placed over the prisoner's wrists and then tightened. The prisoner was made to hang by these rings—this punishment could last

Criminals in Elizabethan England were subject to excruciating punishments including the rack (pictured), which slowly pulled a prisoner's arms and legs out of their sockets.

four or five hours. Gerard was tortured through the use of iron gauntlets. He described his ordeal:

They took me to a big upright pillar, one of the wooden posts that supported the roof of this huge underground chamber. Driven into the top of it were iron staples for supporting heavy weights. Then they put my wrists into iron gauntlets and ordered me to climb two or three wicker steps. My arms were lifted up and an iron bar was passed through the rings of one gauntlet, through the staple, and through the rings of the second gauntlet. This done, they fastened the bar with a pin to prevent it slipping, and then, removing the wicker steps one by one from beneath my feet, they left me hanging by my hands and arms fastened above my head. The tips of my toes, however, still touched the ground and they had to dig away the earth under them. . . .

Sometime after one o'clock, I think, I fell into a faint. How long I was unconscious I don't know, but I do not think it was long, for the men held my body up or put the wicker steps under my feet until I came to. Then they heard me pray and immediately let me down again. They did this every time I fainted—eight or nine times that day—before it struck five.[39]

Drawn and Quartered

As Gerard's treatment illustrates, punishments could be harsh and painful during the Shakespearean era, but nevertheless, England was a country of laws. Those who were imprisoned, tortured, or executed—whether for treason or more common crimes—were accused of violating laws. Those laws had been adopted by Parliament, a lawmaking body whose

After being convicted of treason the Catholic priest Edmund Campion (pictured) was sentenced to a most horrible punishment. He was drawn and quartered, a gruesome penalty even by the harsh standards of Shakespeare's time.

members were popularly elected (although few but the wealthy held the power to vote in Shakespeare's day).

During Shakespeare's era the death penalty was administered for no fewer than two hundred offenses: A pickpocket caught lifting a mere five shillings out of a gentleman's purse could be sentenced to the gallows. Cutting down certain trees was regarded as an act punishable by death. In a typical year during Elizabeth's reign, some eight hundred convicts were put to death.

Executions could be carried out in a number of ways—by hanging, by the axman, or by burning at the stake. The most horrific method of execution was to be drawn and quartered. The hapless defendant was hanged until near death, then taken down and, while still alive, his body parts were hacked off, and finally, the prisoner was disemboweled.

Edmund Campion, a Catholic priest, was drawn and quartered in 1581 along with several others who were convicted of treason. Pronouncing the sentence on Campion and the others, Chief Justice Christopher Wray said:

> You must go to the place from whence you came, there to remain until ye shall be drawn through the open city of London . . . to the place of execution, and there behind and let down alive, and your privy parts cut off, and your entrails taken out and burnt in your sight; then your heads to be cut off, and your bodies to be divided in four parts, to be disposed of at her Majesty's pleasure. And God have mercy on your souls.[40]

Lesser Punishments

Not all criminals were put to death. A criminal convicted of a minor theft—perhaps one involving just a shilling or two—could get off with a sound beating. Another punishment involved use of the pillory—a wooden stand in which a criminal's head and hands were clamped under a bar. He or she was made to stand in a bent, awkward, and painful position for as long as the sentence demanded.

The ducking stool was a punishment reserved for female offenders. The woman was strapped into a wooden armchair that was lifted by a huge arm, then swung over a pond or river. She was then dunked into the water. Depending on the nature of the offense, the woman could be dunked several times or held underwater for a minute or more, bringing her to the brink of drowning. Prostitutes were often sentenced to the ducking stool, but sharp-tongued women whose scoldings were found to be too annoying to be tolerated could find themselves dunked in the Thames. Often dozens or even hundreds of onlookers gathered on the banks of the river or pond to witness the event. Dunkings in Elizabethan England were considered good entertainment. Unlike the tortures carried out in the Tower, the ducking stool was intended more to humiliate the offender than to apply physical punishment.

WORDS IN CONTEXT

ducking stool

A device that hoisted a woman—usually a prostitute or irritating nag—into the air, then submerged her into a river or pond. The punishment was intended to humiliate the offender.

Whippings, on the other hand, were both painful and humiliating as this punishment was carried out in public as well. The hapless criminal sentenced to be "whipped at the cart's tail"[41] was strapped to a horse-drawn cart, often naked, then paraded through the streets of London. Trailing behind were officers of the court who applied lashings as the cart made its way through the streets.

Thieves endured many other forms of punishment. Sometimes holes were burned into their ears or tongues. Other times ears, tongues, and hands were simply hacked off. Branding was another frequently used punishment. In this instance a hot iron was pressed into the cheek of the offender.

A Thriving Trade in Theft

Thievery during the reign of Elizabeth was a thriving trade. Highways outside London offered especially rich pickings for all manner of thieves. One of the most notorious types of thieves of the era was known as an

In Their Own Words

"Put to the Rack"

In 1586 Elizabeth's master spy, Sir Francis Walsingham, informed his monarch that he had uncovered a plot to overthrow her rule. Walsingham obtained the private letters of the queen's cousin, Mary Stuart, Queen of Scots, and is believed to have altered the letters to implicate Mary in a coup organized by a Catholic noble, Anthony Babington. Upon hearing the case against her cousin laid out by Walsingham, Elizabeth flew into a rage. She declared to Walsingham that Mary and her coconspirators be forced to confess—by any means necessary:

> In such cases there is no middle course, we must lay aside clemency and adopt extreme measures. If they shall not seem to you to confess plainly their knowledge, then we warn you cause them to be brought to the rack and first to move them with fear there of . . . then, should the sight of the instrument not induce them to confess, you shall cause them to be put to the rack and to find the taste thereof. . . . Until you shall see fit.

Quoted in Mark P. Donnelly and Daniel Diehl, *The Big Book of Pain: Torture and Punishment Through History.* Gloucestershire, England: History Press, 2012, p. 78.

upright man. He usually led a band of thieves who lurked along the routes in and out of London, ready to pounce on unsuspecting travelers.

Upright men were also known to employ females, known as doxies, who acted as pickpockets at marketplaces and fairs. Girls who were orphaned at young ages and forced to wander the country roads as beggars (or dells) often became doxies. In his 1566 book, *A Caveat of Warning for*

Common Cursitors (during the Elizabethan era, a cursitor was an officer of the court whose duties included drafting arrest warrants) author Thomas Harman explained: "These go [on the road] young, either by the death of their parents and nobody to look unto them, or else by some sharp mistress that they do serve, so they run away. . . . Or she is naturally born one, and then she is a wild dell. These are broken very young when they have been lain with by the upright man then they be doxies and no dells."[42] One scheme used by upright men involved a woman known as a demander for glimmer. She approached a stranger at an ale house, charmed the visitor into giving her small gifts, and promised to meet him later to share the pleasures of the flesh. When the unsuspecting visitor arrived at the destination, he was met by an upright man who relieved the visitor of his purse.

Similar to upright men, rogues also made their livings robbing travelers on the highways, but they usually acted alone and not as the heads of gangs. Some rogues could be unpredictable and prone to violence. They would, for example, approach a person at a fair and beg for a small amount of money. If the victim opened his purse to reveal a large sum, the rogue would likely strike the victim with his staff and steal the purse.

Many thieves were not likely to do harm to their victims. Instead, they preferred the gentler approach—conning their victims out of their money with lies and subterfuge. A whip-jack, for example, usually worked at a fair and claimed to be an out of work sailor. As he told his tall tales of the seafaring life to innocent listeners, he was eyeing nearby stalls and making plans to steal from them. Using even sweeter talk was the well-dressed and well-spoken courtesy man. He made it his duty to greet strangers and join them for drinks. But when the stranger was not looking, the courtesy man snatched his purse.

> **WORDS IN CONTEXT**
> **prigmen**
> Thieves who stole laundered clothes drying on lines or across hedges; prigmen were also chicken thieves.

Petty thieves assumed many guises. Among the pettiest of thieves were the prigmen, who stole laundered clothes drying on lines or across hedges. Prigmen were also chicken thieves. A prigger of prancers was a horse thief. A frater specialized in robbing women as they traveled to and from marketplaces. A toyle was a traveling salesman who over-charged his customers (a crime in the Elizabethan era). A jarkman was a forger. A hooker, also known as an angler, stole possessions from open windows. Another petty thief was a queer-bird, who had just been released from prison and was already planning his next crime. A pal-liard, also known as a clapperdudgeon, was a thief who dressed in the clothes of a beggar so as not to arouse suspicion. One of the tricks of the palliard was to sprawl in the road faking an injury. When a Good Samaritan approached and attempted to give aid to the supposedly injured man, he was robbed.

Like thieves, beggars assumed many roles in order to bleed people of their coins. A counterfeit crank was a man who pretended to suffer from epileptic seizures, known in the era as falling sickness, in order to seek pity from others and ask for alms. The counterfeit crank even went as far as to lather his mouth with soap to make it appear he was suffering from a horrific seizure. Similarly, a dummerer pretended to be unable to speak as a way of finding sympathy. Begging was a crime in Shakespeare's time. To deal with beggars, the authorities often did not bother with the trou-ble of arrest, trial, and imprisonment. Instead, if a beggar was caught, he or she was usually taken to the city limits or edge of the village, beaten, and told not to return.

Corruption in the Courts

If apprehended by the sheriff, thieves of different sorts could hope for fair trials in the English courts. Chances are, though, that the fairness of the judge would depend largely on how much the accused was willing to pay in bribes. Certainly, by Shakespeare's day England was a nation of laws, and the practice of law was a busy profession. By the late 1500s London boasted four law schools: Middle Temple, Inner Temple, Lincoln's Inn, and Gray's Inn—collectively known as the Inns of Court. After educa-tions at Oxford and Cambridge, many gentlemen of the aristocracy en-rolled in law school, and the best graduates expected to be rewarded with seats on the court.

But the courts in England were notoriously corrupt. Judges gladly took bribes, and Elizabeth was not hesitant about firing judges who issued orders she found objectionable. Juries were easily intimidated and jurors easily bribed. Even the young king Edward VI, who ruled briefly after the death of his father, Henry VIII, knew enough about the courts to know they were corrupt. "The lawyers and judges have much offended in corruption and bribery,"[43] the young king wrote in his journal.

WORDS IN CONTEXT

Inns of Court

The four law schools—Middle Temple, Inner Temple, Lincoln's Inn, and Gray's Inn—found in London in the time of Shakespeare.

Shakespeare himself made a wry commentary on the state of English law in his play *Henry VI*. In the play the character Dick the Butcher, a member of a subversive cell, suggests a solution to England's many problems. Says Dick, "The first thing we do, let's kill all the lawyers."[44]

Court of the Star Chamber

Just as few accused offenders could expect to receive fair trials in criminal court, those who filed lawsuits in civil court had little hope of winning their cases. This was especially true when the lawsuit was against a member of the aristocracy. A common merchant who believed an aristocrat had cheated him in a business transaction, for instance, could sue in civil court. A just outcome was highly unlikely, however. Before he was burned at the stake by Mary in 1555, the Church of England bishop Hugh Latimer warned the common people of England they would find no justice against the aristocrats in an English court. "The saying now is, that money is heard every where," wrote Latimer. "If he be rich, he shall soon have an end of his matter. Others are fain to go home with weeping tears, for any help they can obtain at any judges hand. Hear men's suits yourself: put it not to the hearing of these velvet coats; these up-skips."[45]

As corrupt as the common courts in England were, no court was as feared as the Court of the Star Chamber. It was a secret court composed of members of the Privy Council. Often reserved for aristocrats, religious leaders, and others believed to be plotting treacherous acts against the queen, the Star Chamber met behind closed doors, examined only written testimony submitted by witnesses, denied the right of the accused to counsel, employed torture to produce confessions, and invariably

Thieves who were unlucky enough to be caught endured any number of punishments. They might be whipped, branded, burned, or subject to having a hand, ear, or tongue hacked off.

Looking Back

Called Before the Court of the Star Chamber

Woe to the citizen of London called before the Court of the Star Chamber. All the protections under law known to people in modern civilized societies—equal treatment, speedy and public trials, the right to face one's accuser—were unknown in the court, which convened to hear matters of treason and similar crimes against the rule of the monarch. English historian Ian Mortimer explains the functions of the court:

> You should worry if you are summoned to one of its sessions: privy councilors will try you on the basis of written depositions from witnesses—you yourself will not always be allowed to say anything . . . the accused, might be summoned only to hear the judgment. The councilors do not have to abide by the legal system when sentencing you: they can give you any punishment they think fit, from imprisonment in the Tower to whipping, branding, or the pillory. They can punish you by cutting off your ears, slitting your nose, or imposing a heavy fine. There is no jury: every single councilor present is a judge.

Ian Mortimer, *The Time Traveler's Guide to Elizabethan England*. New York: Viking, 2012, p. 262.

returned with verdicts of guilty, pronouncing sentences of death. The Court of the Star Chamber was so named because the pattern of a star was painted on the ceiling of the room where the court convened inside Westminster Palace.

Indeed, when it came to treason against the crown, no degree of bribery could save even the wealthiest aristocrats from the axman. Despite his many accomplishments as a sea captain and explorer, Sir Walter Raleigh was twice imprisoned in the Tower. He was unable to escape his second imprisonment: In 1616, after returning to England from a voyage to Venezuela, Raleigh was arrested and imprisoned because the sailors under his command ransacked a Spanish outpost in the South American country. To appease the Spanish, Raleigh was sentenced to death; he kept his date with the royal executioner on October 29, 1618.

The Court on Trial

But perhaps no case illustrates the corruption of the courts during Shakespeare's era better than the case Elizabeth trumped up against her cousin, Mary Stuart, Queen of Scots. A Catholic, Mary found her rule of Scotland challenged by Protestant nobles who succeeded in overthrowing her reign in 1568. She sought refuge and protection from her cousin Elizabeth in England, who instead suspected Mary of planning a Catholic revolution in England. She detained her cousin at a remote English castle in Chartley, about 140 miles (225 km) north of London, for more than two decades. While Mary was held at Chartley, the Catholic noble Anthony Babington was charged in a plot to assassinate Elizabeth. In 1586 Babington and thirteen conspirators were convicted and drawn and quartered.

Declaring that her imprisoned cousin was in on the plot, Elizabeth put Mary on trial. The evidence used against her included correspondence found in her room at Chartley by Elizabeth's master spy, Sir Francis Walsingham, who is believed to have altered the documents. Mary insisted the letters were forged and that she was innocent. During her trial Mary suggested the English court itself was on trial, and a verdict of guilty would shine a light on a corrupt system of justice. "Look to your consciences," she told the court during her trial, "and remember that the theatre of the whole world is wider than the kingdom of England."[46]

The court aimed to please the queen, and on October 25, 1586, Mary was convicted in the Babington plot. On February 8, 1587, the ax fell across the neck of Mary Stuart.

Mary's execution illustrates that in the England of Shakespeare's day, the corruption of the courts could be felt by anyone. Whether they were aristocrats or cousins to the queen, or whether they were the lowliest of prancers, palliards, and counterfeit cranks, no one was likely to escape the injustices of the law—unless, of course, they could bribe their way out of trouble.

Chapter Five

Life at Sea

England is an island, and for this reason the English have always been in awe of the sea. It was not until the reign of Henry VIII, though, that England built a formidable navy as well as a prosperous merchant fleet. The growth of England as a naval power continued under Elizabeth. In 1588 England became the foremost maritime power on earth when the English navy defeated the Spanish armada off the coast of France. The Spanish king, Phillip II, dispatched his task force of 130 ships to invade England on a religious crusade to return the country to Catholicism, but the plan was thwarted by English warships under the command of Lord Charles Howard and Sir Francis Drake.

Now masters of the world's oceans, the English sailed their ships far across the globe. English merchant ships, naval vessels, privateers, and ships of exploration could be found sailing toward every corner of the planet. In 1599 the English essayist Thomas Nashe described the lure, as well as the danger, of a life at sea:

> Voyages of purchase or reprisals [trading], which are now grown a common traffic, swallow up and consume more sailors and mariners than they breed, and lightly not a slop of a rope-hauler they sent forth to the Queen's ships but he is first broken to the sea in the herring-man's skiff or cockboat, where, having learned to brook all waters, and drink as he can out of a tarry can, and eat poor John [dried salt fish] out of sooty platters, when he may get it, without butter or mustard, there is no "ho" [no stopping] with him, but, once heartened thus, he will needs be a man of war, or a tobacco-taker, and wear a silver whistle. Some of these, for their haughty climbing, come home with wooden legs, and some with none, but leave body and all behind.[47]

Tall Tales

For the young man who toiled on an English farm, struggling behind a plow and a team of oxen, the notion of a life at sea may have seemed both romantic and rewarding. For the lower classes of Shakespeare's era, there was no wealth to be gained at home. Few men born in the poverty of the era could hope to lift themselves out of the fields of dung in which they toiled or the modest cottages they shared with their families. And so it was not unusual for a young man to leave the farm, or the London workhouse, and make his way to the English port cities—Plymouth, Bristol, and Exeter—and join the crew of a merchant vessel, a privateer, or even a voyage of exploration bound for the New World.

Life at sea held great hope. Men who signed on to sail with such captains as Drake or Sir Walter Raleigh could expect to earn high wages and see corners of the world far from their tiny English villages or crowded city streets. Indeed, returning seafarers always had tall tales to tell, which helped entice young and naïve men with the notion that a life at sea was full of adventure.

William Shakespeare helped fuel the notion that sea journeys could lead to strange and exotic lands, most notably in his comedy *The Tempest*. The play tells the story of a ship run aground on a remote Mediterranean island due to a storm—a tempest—stirred up magically by the island's inhabitant, Prospero. As three characters, Antonio, Gonzolo, and Sebastian, explore the island, they describe their exotic environment:

Gonzalo: How lush and lusty the grass looks! How green!
Antonio: The ground, indeed, is tawny!
Sebastian: With an eye of green in't.[48]

For a young Londoner standing among the stinkards in the Globe Theatre, pressing flowers into his nose to avoid the odors of the city and wiping horse dung off his shoes, the lusty grass and tawny fields described by Shakespeare must surely have seemed inviting. In real-

In a scene from The Tempest, *sailors are amazed at the creatures they encounter after washing up in an unfamiliar land following a shipwreck. In writing the play, Shakespeare capitalized on the widely held view that a sailor's life was filled with adventure.*

ity, though, things were not always as pleasant as Antonio, Sebastian, and Gonzalo found on Prospero's island. Returning to England from Nova Scotia in 1568, the sailor Davy Ingram reported that he had encountered cannibals, strange beasts, and Native American tribesmen whose brutality was beyond comprehension. Ingram told his lively and likely embellished account to his appalled listeners: "When any of them is sicke and like to die [the] next of kinne doe cut his throte and all his kinne must drinke up his bloude."[49]

Ingram's audience in the local tavern may have listened to his story with a sense of disgust. On the other hand, they undoubtedly pricked up their ears when he also reported seeing nuggets of gold and silver "as bigge as his fyst" while women of the native tribes wore "plates of gold all over their body."[50]

Not all men went to sea willingly. With the English navy expanding its fleet, challenging the Spanish with greater frequency, and sailing

WORDS IN CONTEXT

impressment

The recruitment of men against their will by the English navy for duty aboard warships.

to more remote destinations, captains often found themselves short of crew members. In 1563 Elizabeth approved a law permitting the impressment of young men into the English navy; essentially, English citizens could be drafted for maritime service. Moreover, in 1597 Parliament approved the Vagrancy Act, enabling the navy to force able-bodied yet unemployed men to serve aboard ships.

Wealth of Far-Off Lands

Still, seafarers with more credibility than Ingram could be counted on to tell stories of wealth waiting to be scooped up by anyone willing to put to sea. Returning from the South American country Guyana in 1596, Raleigh had this to say about what he found:

> The empire of Guiana is directly east from Peru towards the sea, and lieth under the equinoctial line, and it hath more abundance of gold than any part of Peru, and as many or more great cities than ever Peru had when it flourished most. . . . I have been assured by such of the Spaniards as have seen Manoa the imperial city of Guiana, which the Spaniards call El Dorado, that for the greatness, for the riches, and for the excellent seat, it far exceedeth any of the world. . . . Undoubtedly those that trade Amazon return much gold.[51]

But the apparent wealth in far-off lands waiting for the seafaring traveler was only one way to reap booty from a life on the waves. Drake, Raleigh, and numerous other swashbuckling captains were privateers—essentially, pirates—and shared their plunder with their crew members. Indeed, in 1577 Drake set sail on a circumnavigation of the earth—an awe-inspiring mission of exploration and discovery.

It was also a mission guaranteed to fill the pockets of Drake and his men as well as enrich the personal fortune of the queen, to whom Drake

In Their Own Words

John Hawkins, Slaver

In 1562 an English navy admiral, John Hawkins, arrived on the coast of Sierra Leone in West Africa, where he captured slaves. Hawkins was among the first to see the value of capturing Africans and selling them as slaves in the New World. His missions were, in fact, financed by Elizabeth, who shared in his profits. In 1598 the English writer Richard Hakluyt recounted one of Hawkins's slaving expeditions:

> The captain, who with a dozen men went through the town, returned, finding 200 negroes at the water's side shooting at them in the boats, and cutting them in pieces which were drowned in the water. Thus we returned back somewhat discomforted, although captain in a singular wise manner carried himself with countenance very cheerful outwardly, having gotten by our going ten negroes, and lost seven of our best man, and we had 27 of our men hurt.
>
> We departed with all our ships from Sierra Leone towards the West Indies, and for the space of eighteen days we were becalmed, having now and then contrary winds, which happen to us very ill, being but reasonably watered for so great a company of negroes and ourselves, which pinched us all, and that which was worst, put us in such fear that many never thought to have reached to the Indies without great death of negroes and of themselves.

Quoted in R.E. Pritchard, *Shakespeare's England: Life in Elizabethan and Jacobean Times.* Gloucestershire, England: Sutton, 1999, p. 234.

was beholden to share the booty. Setting sail with five ships under his command, Drake soon encountered and attacked six Spanish and Portuguese merchant vessels. In addition to looting the vessels, Drake seized one of the Portuguese ships, placed it under his command, and continued his voyage around the world.

The rest of the voyage went less smoothly. Drake suspected one of the captains under his command, Thomas Doughty, of plotting against him. Drake had the captain executed and his ship burned. When the four remaining ships entered the Strait of Magellan at the southern tip of the South American continent, they encountered bad weather and lost one of their ships. Drake abandoned another ship because too many sailors were sick with disease or weak from hunger to man all the vessels. He took the survivors aboard the two remaining ships: his own, the *Golden Hind*, and that of captain John Wynter, the *Elizabeth*. At that point Wynter decided the mission was doomed

Despite numerous setbacks and misadventures, Sir Francis Drake circumnavigated the globe in his sailing ship Golden Hind. *A replica of Drake's ship is pictured below.*

and returned to England, leaving only Drake's vessel to continue the circumnavigation.

Undaunted, Drake headed north and sailed along the coast of Chile, attacking every Spanish vessel he encountered while sending his men ashore to loot villages along the coast. Finally, after getting his fill of all Chile had to offer, Drake headed west and across the Pacific. Along the way he encountered numerous other mishaps, such as running aground near some Pacific islands. Three years after setting sail, the *Golden Hind* limped back into port in Plymouth, England.

Hard Work and Harsh Conditions

As Drake's voyage illustrates, conditions aboard ship could be harsh. Space was tight. The typical cabin featured a ceiling no more than 5 feet 8 inches (1.7 m) high. Belowdecks, tall sailors were forced to crouch for the entire voyage. Even crew members of diminutive stature lacked comfort: There was simply not enough space for cargo, cannons, supplies, and men to share. Men were forced to sleep on hard wooden decks, shoulder to shoulder—although hammocks were introduced in 1596. Any sailor forced to rise at night to visit the ship's privy was sure to be cursed as he stepped over his shipmates, undoubtedly rousing them from their much-needed slumber. And there was, of course, water everywhere. A sailor could expect to spend the entire voyage in damp clothes—a condition that lent itself to disease.

The work was hard. Sailors toiled from dawn until after dusk. There was always something that needed to be done aboard ship—cleaning the deck, attending to the riggings, stowing or raising the sails, mending ropes, catching fish, keeping the timbers caulked to prevent leaks. Sailors were given time off in the evenings, which they usually spent relaxing, playing cards, or making music with fiddles and pipes.

Spoiled Food and Disease

Fresh food was a rare luxury aboard ship. Saturating meat in salt could preserve the meat for a time, but eventually the meat turned rancid. Bread grew stale quickly, and so the ship's cook constantly baked fresh loaves. But keeping the flour from growing mold was a challenge in itself. Also, flour was often infected by vermin aboard the ship, particularly weevils. For an English sailor, a typical day's meal consisted of a gallon (3.8 L) of beer, a pound (454 g) of biscuits or bread, half a pound (227 g) of cheese, 4 ounces (113 g) of butter, and half a pound of either meat or fish. Upon joining the crew, each man was issued a wooden bowl and wooden spoon, which he used for meals. He ate aboard ship wherever he could, squatting on whatever open deck space he could find. Depending on the quality of what the cook served that day—and many weeks or months after the voyage commenced, the cook may have been forced to serve spoiled meat and moldy bread—the mate might very well elect to toss his supper overboard.

> **WORDS IN CONTEXT**
>
> **scurvy**
>
> A disease that afflicted seafarers due to the lack of vitamin C in their diets; it was often fatal.

The disease known as scurvy was always an enemy. The disease, which could be deadly, was caused by lack of vitamin C. Storing fruits and vegetables, the best source of vitamin C, aboard ships was usually impossible—they rotted over the course of a long voyage. In 1596 the English sea surgeon William Clowes described the effects of scurvy on his shipmates:

> Their gums were rotten even to the very roots of their very teeth, and their cheeks hard and swollen, the teeth were loose neere ready to fall out. . . . Their breath a filthy savour. The legs were feeble and so weak, that they were not scarce able to carrie their bodies. Moreover they were full of aches and paines, with many blewish and reddish staines or spots, some broad and some small like flea-biting.[52]

Another ship's surgeon of the era, writing anonymously, concluded there was often little hope for the scurvy victim. "Many of our people died of it every day, and we saw bodies thrown into the sea constantly, three or four at the time," he wrote. "For the most part they died without aid given them, expiring behind some case or chest, their eyes and soles of their feet gnawed away by the rats."[53]

Officers usually did not suffer from scurvy. Whatever fruits could be kept fresh were saved for the captain's table, which he shared with his fellow officers. Indeed, the officers invited into the captain's cabin to dine with the ship's master may have seen fresh fruits such as grapes, plums, apples, and pears served on pewter plates. The captain and his officers also enjoyed flagons of wine.

Other ailments afflicted the men at sea. One was dysentery—a form of diarrhea so severe that the men's stool contained blood. Dysentery victims also ran high fevers, and many died. Dysentery was caused by food or

The disease of scurvy, symptoms of which are pictured, commonly afflicted English sailors during long sea voyages. Scurvy resulted from a lack of fresh fruits and vegetables containing the vitamin C that prevents the illness.

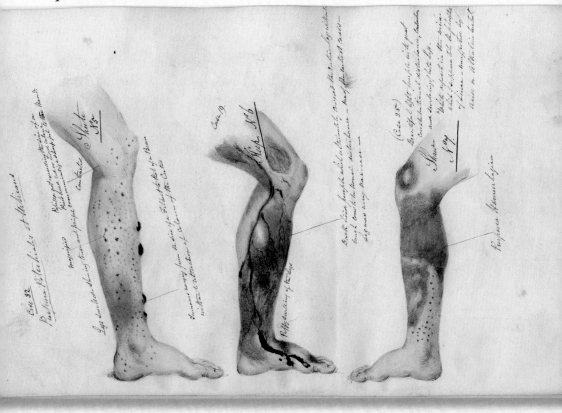

water fouled with bacteria—a common occurrence aboard ship because sanitation and personal hygiene were virtually nonexistent. Other ills afflicting men at sea were tooth decay and gum disease, which caused them to lose teeth; diseases caused by infestation of their dirty clothes or hair by fleas, beetles, and other insects; and diseases that were spawned by the ship's filthy privies—usually holes in the deck covered with removable planks. (Officers were privileged to be issued their own chamber pots.)

Death and Discipline Aboard Ship

Disease took so many lives that it was not unusual for a captain to complete a voyage with half the men he started with—a sad fact, given that crew members could be boys as young as ten or eleven. The chances of a seafaring lad reaching adulthood were decidedly slim.

If disease did not cost a crew member his life, he faced other perils. Sometimes the Spaniards won the ship-to-ship combat, meaning the English sailor could very well lose his life in battle. Shipwrecks were common; sailors rarely survived them. And swashbucklers such as Drake and Raleigh were not the only pirates on the high seas—the Barbary pirates, rogue sailors who haunted the Mediterranean Sea off the coast of North Africa, were a particular danger.

> **WORDS IN CONTEXT**
> **keelhaul**
> A punishment inflicted on sailors in which the victim was hauled under the ship's keel, where he invariably succumbed to drowning.

There were numerous other ways to find one's life at sea cut short. Falling overboard, particularly during a storm, was always a danger. So was committing an infraction of the rules. Discipline aboard ship was strict: floggings were administered for such violations as using objectionable language, drunkenness, and sleeping on duty, with the number of lashes dependent on the seriousness of the offense. Much more serious offenses were punished with much more serious measures: A thief was tarred and feathered; a killer lashed to his victim's body and tossed overboard. Drawing a knife on a shipmate could cost the sailor his hand. At the captain's discretion, a mate could be keel-hauled: The sailor's hands and feet were lashed to long ropes, then he was thrown overboard. His body was dragged under the ship's bottom, torn apart by the sharp barnacles that attached themselves to the vessel. No one was expected to survive the ordeal of the keelhaul.

The Voyage of Henry Hudson

Sometimes it was the captain—and not the crew members—whose luck turned ill aboard ship. Mutinies were not common—and when they did occur, crew members were often dealt with harshly when they returned to England. Nevertheless, sometimes the captain pushed his men too far, meted out too many floggings, failed to provide them enough food, or failed to reward them with the riches they expected by making the voyage.

Or, as in the case of English explorer Henry Hudson, mutiny resulted when the crew blamed their captain for making bad decisions that endangered their lives. Over the course of three voyages starting in 1607, Hudson explored the Chesapeake, Delaware, and New York bays and became the first European to sail up what is today known as the Hudson River in New York. In April 1610 Hudson embarked on his fourth and final voyage west, attempting to find the Northwest Passage to Asia through Arctic waters. By November Hudson's ship, the *Discovery*, was mired in ice in what is today known as the Hudson Bay in Canada. His men were forced to camp ashore, where they weathered a brutally cold winter. By the time the weather broke in the spring, the men were near starvation and blamed their captain for their predicament. They felt no desire to return to the *Discovery* and continue the mission under Hudson's command, and so they mutinied. Hudson and eight others who remained loyal, including Hudson's teenage son John, were set adrift in a small boat. The nine were never seen again.

As Hudson and his loyal men were rounded up by the mutineers, one of those who stayed loyal, a carpenter named Philip Staffe, is said to have asked the mutineers, "Will you be hanged when you get home?"[54] As it turned out, the mutineers were spared the gallows. The naval authorities were slow to bring charges against the mutineers—evidently because the crew members related that they had, in fact, found the Northwest Passage.

Looking Back

The Fate of Henry Hudson

According to University of Southern California history professor Peter C. Mancall, there is little to suggest that Henry Hudson did not anticipate the treacherous Canadian winter in 1610—the circumstance that led to the mutiny of his crew. Hudson had explored the region before, was an expert mariner, and was well aware of the harshness of the season should his ship become mired in ice—which it did. Says Mancall:

> At the time of his fourth voyage in 1610, no English mariner of the age knew the North Atlantic as well as Henry Hudson. His boldness in leading ships northward season after season had revealed him as a man willing to take risks in the effort to explore new territory and bring home both hard-won knowledge and the promise of profit. Remarkably, none of Hudson's men perished on his expeditions of 1607 and 1608. He had proved he knew what it took for his men to survive. . . .
>
> He acknowledged and anticipated the terrors that shrouded the Arctic once the sun, perpetually visible during the prime sailing months, made its inevitable dip below the horizon and virtually disappeared for months. The darkness that followed could seem inescapable to those unfamiliar with northern rhythms. Ship candles and oil lamps provided small solace in an enduring gloom that, for those trapped in ice and snared by darkness, could feel like in interminable prison sentence, one that could incite despondency, fury, and madness.

Peter C. Mancall, *Fatal Journey: The Final Expedition of Henry Hudson.* New York: Basic Books, 2009, p. 3.

Since this information was too important to be lost through the sentence of execution, Hudson's crew members were permitted to remain free after their return, and in fact, two crewmen returned to Hudson Bay during later voyages. All mutineers died of natural causes.

Finding Paradise

The ordeal of Hudson's men illustrates, however, that despite Shakespeare's claim that sea travel could reward crew members with visits to exotic lands, the reality was much different. Life at sea could be dangerous, and few crew members lived to see the hoped-for wealth.

But harsh conditions were common for most people living in the England of Shakespeare's day. City dwellers toiled in the crafts and trades or as vendors, often living in squalid conditions and fending off thieves. Farm life was filled with backbreaking labor and little opportunity to gain wealth. Only the aristocrats could truly enjoy the benefits of life in their times—but even being an aristocrat held perils. Those who insulted the queen, uttered the wrong words at court, or otherwise fell out of favor could lose their freedom or their head.

Through it all, though, England prospered during the time of Shakespeare. The country became an economic and maritime power as well as a leader in literature—evidence of which is found in the prodigious works of Shakespeare himself. And in 1607, nine years before the playwright's death, the first English settlers arrived in the Jamestown colony in Virginia. They brought a strong measure of English life to the New World, providing a foothold for the culture of their home in America. Writing in 1619, the English poet Michael Drayton urged his countrymen to seek new lives in America:

And cheerfully at sea
Success you still entice
To get the pearl and gold,
And ours to hold,
Virginia,
Earth's only paradise.[55]

Many people took Drayton's advice and sought new lives in the New World, establishing colonies not only in Virginia but soon in Massachusetts, Pennsylvania, and elsewhere. And they brought with them many aspects of their culture. Until the American Revolution of 1776, the colonies were ruled by England; therefore, the citizens abided by English laws. Tradespeople made their livings in cities like Boston and Philadelphia just as they had in London. Thieves were flogged and other punishments were meted out as well—Boston, New York, and Philadelphia all had their ducking stools. Great ports were established, where English ships and their crewmen arrived daily. And libraries and theaters were established as well, providing the residents of the New World opportunities to laugh and cry at the fates of the characters who populated the plays of Shakespeare.

Source Notes

Introduction: Afternoons at the Globe Theatre

1. Quoted in R.E. Pritchard, *Shakespeare's England: Life in Elizabethan and Jacobean Times.* Gloucestershire, England: Sutton, 1999, p. 188.
2. Quoted in Will Durant, *The Age of Reason Begins: The Story of Civilization*, vol. 7. New York: Simon & Schuster, 1961, p. 105.

Chapter One: The Queen and Her Court

3. Quoted in Durant, *The Age of Reason Begins*, p. 3.
4. Quoted in A.N. Wilson, *The Elizabethans.* New York: Farrar, Straus and Giroux, 2011, p. 29.
5. William Shakespeare, *Richard III*, Massachusetts Institute of Technology, 1993. http://shakespeare.mit.edu.
6. Quoted in Christian History, "John Foxe," August 8, 2008. www.christianitytoday.com.
7. Quoted in Sara Mendelson and Patricia Crawford, *Women in Early Modern England, 1550–1720.* Oxford: Clarendon, 1998, p. 349.
8. Quoted in Wilson, *The Elizabethans*, p. 41.
9. Quoted in Durant, *The Age of Reason Begins*, p. 13.
10. Quoted in Durant, *The Age of Reason Begins*, p. 9.
11. Quoted in John Nichols, *The Progresses and Public Processions of Queen Elizabeth.* New York: Bert Franklin, 1823, p. iv.
12. Quoted in Carolly Erickson, *The First Elizabeth.* New York: St. Martin's, 1983, p. 282.
13. Quoted in Anna Jameson, *Memoirs of Celebrated Female Sovereigns.* New York: Harper, 1832, pp. 235–36.
14. Quoted in J.W. Allen, *A History of Political Thought in the 16th Century.* New York: Routledge, 2010, p. 127.

15. Quoted in Ilona Bell, *Elizabeth I: The Voice of a Monarch.* New York: Palgrave MacMillan, 2010, p. 111.

16. Quoted in Wilson, *The Elizabethans*, p. 373.

Chapter Two: Language and Learning in Shakespeare's Day

17. Quoted in Gerald Suster, ed., *John Dee.* Berkeley, CA: North Atlantic, 2003, p. 119.

18. Quoted in Katya Gifford, "The English Language During the Elizabethan Age," HumanitiesWeb.org, June 10, 2002. www.humanitiesweb .org.

19. Quoted in Ronald A. Wells, *Dictionaries and the Authoritarian Tradition.* The Hague, Netherlands: Mouton, 1973, p. 17.

20. Quoted in Wells, *Dictionaries and the Authoritarian Tradition*, p. 17.

21. Quoted in Pritchard, *Shakespeare's England*, pp. 88–89.

22. Quoted in Wilson, *The Elizabethans*, p. 78.

23. Quoted in Wilson, *The Elizabethans*, p. 79.

24. Quoted in Pritchard, *Shakespeare's England*, p. 92.

25. Quoted in Pritchard, *Shakespeare's England*, p. 98.

26. Quoted in Pritchard, *Shakespeare's England*, p. 101.

Chapter Three: City Life and Country Life

27. Quoted in Pritchard, *Shakespeare's England*, p. 156.

28. William Harrison, *The Description of England: The Classic Contemporary Account of Tudor Social Life.* Mineola, NY: Dover, 1994, p. 399.

29. Harrison, *The Description of England*, p. 398.

30. Quoted in Ian Mortimer, *The Time Traveler's Guide to Elizabethan England.* New York: Viking, 2012, p. 123.

31. Quoted in Mortimer, *The Time Traveler's Guide to Elizabethan England*, p. 236.

32. Quoted in Pritchard, *Shakespeare's England*, p. 175.

33. Quoted in Elizabethan Era, "Elizabethan Bull & Bear Baiting," 2014. www.elizabethan-era.org.uk.

34. Quoted in Wilson, *The Elizabethans*, p. 307.

35. William Shakespeare, *As You Like It*, Massachusetts Institute of Technology, 1993. http://shakespeare.mit.edu.

36. Quoted in Pritchard, *Shakespeare's England*, p. 69.

37. Quoted in Pritchard, *Shakespeare's England*, p. 70.

Chapter Four: Crime and Punishment

38. Quoted in Mark P. Donnelly and Daniel Diehl, *The Big Book of Pain: Torture and Punishment Through History*. Gloucestershire, England: History Press, 2012, p. 10.

39. Quoted in Mortimer, *The Time Traveler's Guide to Elizabethan England*, pp. 74–75.

40. Quoted in Richard Simpson, *Edmund Campion: A Biography*. London: Hodges, 1896, p. 436.

41. Quoted in Jean Kellaway, *The History of Torture and Execution: From Early Civilization Through Medieval Times to the Present*. Guilford, CT: Lyons, 2003, p. 67.

42. Quoted in Mortimer, *The Time Traveler's Guide to Elizabethan England*, p. 265.

43. Quoted in Sharon Turner, *The History of England from the Reigns of Edward the Sixth, Mary and Elizabeth*. London: Longman, Rees, Orme, Brown, Green and Longman, 1835, p. 279.

44. William Shakespeare, *Henry VI*, Massachusetts Institute of Technology, 1993. http://shakespeare.mit.edu.

45. Quoted in Turner, *The History of England from the Reigns of Edward the Sixth, Mary and Elizabeth*, p. 280.

46. Quoted in Robert Stedall, *The Survival of the Crown*. Brighton, England: Book Guild, 2014, p. 233.

Chapter Five: Life at Sea

47. Quoted in Pritchard, *Shakespeare's England*, p. 231.

48. William Shakespeare, *The Tempest*, Massachusetts Institute of Technology, 1993. http://shakespeare.mit.edu.

49. Quoted in Wilson, *The Elizabethans*, p. 219.

50. Quoted in Wilson, *The Elizabethans*, p. 219.

51. Quoted in Pritchard, *Shakespeare's England*, p. 237.

52. Quoted in Stephen R. Bown, *Scurvy: How a Surgeon, a Mariner, and a Gentleman Solved the Greatest Medical Mystery of the Age of Sail.* New York: St. Martin's, 2003, p. 34.

53. Quoted in Brown, *Scurvy*, p. 34.

54. Quoted in Peter C. Mancall, *Fatal Journey: The Final Expedition of Henry Hudson*: New York: Basic Books, 2009, p. 128.

55. Quoted in Pritchard, *Shakespeare's England*, p. 245.

For Further Research

Books

Jessie Childs, *God's Traitors: Terror and Faith in Elizabethan England.* New York: Oxford University Press, 2014.

David Ellis, *The Truth About William Shakespeare: Fact, Fiction and Modern Biographies.* Edinburgh, Scotland: Edinburgh University Press, 2012.

Nigel Jones, *Tower: An Epic History of the Tower of London.* New York: St. Martin's, 2012.

Stuart A. Kallen, *Elizabethan England.* San Diego, CA: ReferencePoint, 2013.

Ian Mortimer, *The Time Traveler's Guide to Elizabethan England.* New York: Viking, 2012.

David Robson, *Shakespeare's Globe Theater.* San Diego, CA: ReferencePoint, 2014.

Susan Ronald, *Heretic Queen: Queen Elizabeth I and the Wars of Religion.* New York: St. Martin's, 2012.

A.N. Wilson, *The Elizabethans.* New York: Farrar, Straus and Giroux, 2012.

Websites

Complete Works of William Shakespeare (http://shakespeare.mit .edu). The Massachusetts Institute of Technology created this online archive of all the plays and sonnets written by Shakespeare.

Elizabethan Era (www.elizabethan-era.org.uk). Authored by British historian and writer Linda Alchin, the site contains an enormous amount of background on life in Elizabethan England. Topics covered include education, theater, apparel, architecture, wars, diet, city life, country life, and many other areas of study.

First Flushing Toilet (http://bathtubhistory.wordpress.com/2009/07 /02/bathtub-ancient-history-tales-of-the-bathtub/oldtoilet). The story of how Sir John Harrington, godson to Queen Elizabeth I, invented the first flushing toilet is told on this website. The site includes a photo of the commode and a narrative of how Harrington was mocked by critics.

Golden Hind (www.goldenhind.co.uk). A replica of the *Golden Hind*, the ship sailed around the world by Sir Francis Drake, is on display in Devon, England. Visitors to the website can take a virtual tour of the ship that includes many photographs as well as the log of the voyage kept by Drake.

Piracy and Privateering with Elizabethan Maritime Expansion (www .nps.gov/fora/forteachers/piracy-and-privateering-with-elizabethan -maritime-expansion.htm). Maintained by the National Park Service for the Fort Raleigh National Historic Site in North Carolina, the website provides a narrative of privateering by English pirates along the American coastline during the Elizabethan era. Students can find journal entries by sailors who encountered privateers.

William Shakespeare (www.bbc.co.uk/history/people/william_shake speare). Maintained by the BBC, the website includes an extensive biography of history's greatest dramatist. Links on the page will lead students to a biography of Queen Elizabeth I, an archive of portraits of Shakespeare, and podcasts of BBC radio shows in which historians explain the life and times of Shakespeare.

Index

Note: Boldface page numbers indicate illustrations.

absentee landlords, 49
actors, 11
alchemy, defined, 27
anglers, 65
apprenticeships, 34
aristocracy
    corruption in courts and, 66
    education of, 31–32
    Elizabeth and
        court of, 22, 24–25
        favor of, 83
        as Privy Council members, 20
    as farm owners, 49
    grand tour, 39–40
    marriage among, 34
As You Like It (Shakespeare), 53

Babington, Anthony, 63, 69
Bacon, Sir Francis, 25, 31, 39–40
bathing, 47–48
bearbaiting, 52
beggars, 65
Bloody Mary, 12, 16
    See also Mary (queen of England)
Boleyn, Anne, 14, 15
Book of Husbandry (Fitzherbert), 55
books
    dissolution of Catholic Church and, 27–28
    hornbook, 33
    in library of Dee, 27
    printing press, 28, **29**
Bosworth, Battle of (1485), 13
branding, 62
bribery, 25, 66
brothels, 52
bubonic plague, 48, 50, **51**
bullbaiting, 52

Calvin, John, 15
Cambridge, 37, 38
Camden, William, 26
Campion, Edmund, **60**, 61
Catherine of Aragon, 14–15
Catholic Church. *See* Roman Catholic Church

Caveat of Warning for Common Cursitors, A (Harman), 63–64
Cawdrey, Robert, 30–31
Caxton, William, 28–30, **29**
Cecil, William, 19, 20
chamber pots, 47–48
chapmen, defined, 42
children, employment of, 47
Church of England
    and education of clergy, 38
    established, 15, 27
    prayerbook for, 25
cities
    number and population range of, 41
    See also London
clapperdudgeons, 65
cleanliness, 47–48
Clement VII (pope), 15
clergy, education of, 38
Clowes, William, 78
cockfights, 50
colonization, 83–84
comedies (by Shakespeare)
    As You Like It, 53
    described, 10
    Tempest, The, 72, **73**
commerce, 56
companies, 45
counterfeit cranks, 65
country squires, 49
courtesy men, 64
Court of the Star Chamber, 66–68
courts, 65–68
crime
    begging as, 65
    and corruption in judicial system, 65–66
    thievery as, 62–63, 64–65, **67**
    See also punishment
crops, 54

dame schools, 32–33
death penalty, 61
Dee, John, 27
Dekker, Thomas, 41, 48, 50
dictionary, first English, 30–31
Discovery (ship), 81

disease(s)
    afflicting sailors, 78–80, **79**
    bubonic plague, 48, 50, **51**
    falling sickness, 65
Doxies, 63–64
Drake, Sir Francis
    as privateer circumnavigating globe, 72, 74, **76**,
        76–77
    Spanish armada and, 71
drawing and quartering, **60**, 61
Drayton, Michael, 83
ducking stools, 62
Dudley, Robert, 19
dummerers, 65
dysentery, 79–80

Earle, John, 38–39
education
    of aristocracy, 31–32
    boarding school, 34–35
    of clergy, 38
    and discipline, 36, **36**, 37
    of farm children, 34
    of girls, 34, 35
    grammar school, 33–34
    law school, 65, 66
    petty (dame) school, 32–33, 34
    of poor children, 34
    and school layout, 35–36, **36**
    of Shakespeare, 32
    university, 37–39
Edward VI (king of England), 15, 25, 66
Elizabeth (ship), 76–77
Elizabethan era, 11
Elizabeth I (queen of England), **18**
    birth of, 15
    coronation of, 12–13
    court of, 22, 24–25, **32**
    death of, 26
    marriage and, 18–19, 20, 21
    personality of, 19
    popularity of, 11, 19–20, 22, 26
    reign of, 11
        England as naval power during, 71
        Parliament during, 25–26
        Privy Council during, 20
        progresses by, 22–24, **23**
        promises made about, 17
        on rule by woman, 19
        serfdom outlawed by, 53
    during reign of Mary, 12, 16
Elyot, Thomas, 16, 18, 31
employment, 45, 47
England, **14,** 41
English language, 28–31
entertainment, 50–53, 62

Eton, 34
executions, 61

fabric factories, 47
factories, 47
farmers and education, 34
fires, 50
Fitzherbert, Sir Anthony, 55
flush toilets, 48
food, 55
forgers, 65
Forman, Simon, 48
Foxe, John, 16
fraters, 64–65

gambling, 50
Gerard, John, 57, 59–60
girls
    education of, 34, 35
    employment of, 47
    marriage of aristocratic, 34
Globe Theatre, 8–10, **9**
Golden Hind (ship), **76**, 76–77
Gosson, Stephen, 10
Governour, The (Elyot), 31
grammar schools, 33–34
grand tour, 39–40
Great Fire of London (1666), 43, 50
Great Plague (1665), 50
groundlings, 9–10
Gutenberg, Johannes, 28

Hakluyt, Richard, 75
Harman, Thomas, 63–64
Harrington, Sir John, 48
Harrison, William, 44, 45
Hatfield castle, 12, 16, 17
Hawkins, John, 75
Hayward, John, 19
Henry VI (Shakespeare), 66
Henry VII (king of England), 13
Henry VIII (king of England)
    Catholic Church and, 13–15, 19, 27
    English navy and, 71
heretic, defined, 19
heretics, 58
histories (by Shakespeare), 11, 66
Holy Inquisition, 58
homes, 54
hookers, 65
hornbooks, 33
horses, 47
House of Tudor, 13
House of York, 13
Howard, Lord Charles, 71
Hudson, Henry, 81–83

hygiene, 47–48, 54

illiteracy, 31
impressment, defined, 74
industrialization, 46–47
Ingram, Davy, 73
inns, 42, 43–45, **44**
Inns of Court, 65, 66
inn-yards, 42
Inquisition, 58
iron gauntlets, 58–60

jakes, 48
James I (king of England), 26
Jameson, Anna, 25
Jamestown colony in Virginia, 83
jarkmen, 65
jousting, 50–51

keelhaul, 80–81

Laneham, Robert, 52
Latimer, Hugh, 66
law schools, 65, 66
Leicester, Earl of (Robert Dudley), 19
Lily, William, 33
literacy, 31
London
    bubonic plague in, 48, 50, **51**
    commerce in, 56
    described, 41–42
    entering, 42, **44**
    entertainment in, 50–52
    Globe Theatre and, 8–10, **9**
    Great Fire in, 43
    industry in, 46–47
    inns in, 42, 43–45, **44**
    law schools in, 65, 66
    London Bridge and, 43
    marketplaces in, 45, **46**
    odors in, 47
    poor in, 8
    population growth in, 53
    Strand in, 42
    Tower of London and, 57
    Westminster district of, 42
Luther, Martin, 15

Mancall, Peter C., 82
marriage, 34
Mary (queen of England)
    death of, 12
    marriage of, to Phillip, 18, 19
    Privy Council of, 20
    religion and, 15–16
Mary Stuart (Queen of Scots), 63, 69–70

masters, 33
McMurtry, Jo, 21, 49
Metamorphosis of Ajax, The (Harrington), 48
Mortimer, Ian, 38, 68
Moryson, Fynes, 43
Mulcaster, Richard, 35, 36

Nashe, Thomas, 71
nobility. *See* aristocracy

Odyssey, The, 23
Oxford, 37, 38

palliards, 65
Parliament, 25–26, 60–61
Peasant's Revolt (1381), 53
petty schools, 32–33, 34
Phillip II (king of Spain), 16, 71
pillory, 61
Pit, the, 58
plague, 48, 50, **51**
poor people, 8, 34
Pope, Alexander, 23
prigmen, 64
printing press, 28, **29**
privateers, 74, 76
Privy Council, 20, 66
progresses, 22–24, **23**
prompters, 37
prostitution, 52, 62
Protestant Reformation, 15
punishment
    death penalty as, 61
    imposed by Court of the Star Chamber, 68
    lesser, 61–62, **67**
    at sea, 80–81
    and use of torture, 57–60, **59**, **60**

queer-birds, 65
quilting, 53
quintain, 51

rack, 58, **59**
Raleigh, Sir Walter, 72, 74
Reformation, 15
religion
    of Church of England
        and education of clergy, 38
        established, 15, 27
        prayerbook for, 25
    education and, 33
    Edward I and, 25
    Elizabeth and, 19–20
    Henry VIII and Catholic Church, 13–15, 19, 27
    Mary (queen of England) and, 15–16
    Mary Stuart and, 63, 69–70

Roman Catholic Church, 15
  Spanish armada and, 71
Richard II (king of England), 53
Richard III (Shakespeare), 13
Rishton, Edward, 58
rogues, 64
Roman Catholic Church
  books and manuscripts owned by, 27–28
  Elizabeth and, 19–20
  English subjects and, 19
  Henry VIII and, 13–15, 19, 27
  Holy Inquisition of, 58
  Reformation and, 15
romances (plays), 11
royal progresses, 22–24, **23**
rural life
  absentee landlords and, 49
  described, 34, 54–55
  entertainment in, 53
  and homes, 54

sanitation, 47–48, 50, 54
scavenger's daughter, 57
scriveners, 33
scurvy, 78–79, **79**
scythes, described, 55
seafaring
  deaths, 80–81
  English navy, 71, 73–74
  literature about, 72–73, **73**
  lure of, 71–73
  mutinies, 81–83
  shipboard conditions
    and discipline and punishments,
      80–81
    and diseases, 78–80, **79**
    and food, 77–78, 79
    and living areas, 77
    and work tasks, 77
serfdom/serfs, 53
Seymour, Jane, 15
Shakespeare, William, **9, 32**
  education of, 32
  plays by, 10–11
    As You Like It, 53
    Henry VI, 66
    Richard III, 13
    Tempest, The (Shakespeare), 72, **73**
  spelling of name of, 31
sickles, described, 55
Sidney, Philip, 39
Sixtus V (pope), 19–20
slavery, 75

Spanish armada (1588), 71
spelling, 31
sports, 50–52
Staffe, Philip, 81
Star Chamber, 66–68
Stephens, John, 54
Stuart, Mary (Queen of Scots), 63, 69–70
switches, 36, **36**, 37

Table Alphabeticall, A (Cawdrey), 30–31
Tempest, The (Shakespeare), 72, **73**
textbooks, 33
Thames River, 43, 48
toilets, 48
torture instruments, 57–61, **59**, **60**
Tower of London, 57
toyles, 65
trades and crafts, 45, **46**
tragedies (by Shakespeare), 10
Tudor, House of, 13
tutors, 34, 37

university, 37–39
upright men, 63
ushers, 33, 34

Vagrancy Act (1597), 74
Virgin Queen. *See* Elizabeth I (queen of England)

Walsingham, Sir Francis, 20, 63, 69
Wars of the Roses (1455–1485), 13
wealthy
  overview of life of , 8
  See also aristocracy
whip-jacks, 64
whippings, 62
Willis, R., 37
Winchester, 34
women
  acting and, 11
  criminals, 63–64
  death of, in childbirth, 19
  employment of, 47
  farmwives, 54–55
  as leaders, 16, 18
  prostitutes, 62
  punishments for, 62
workhouses, defined, 8
Wray, Christopher, 61
Wyatt, Sir Thomas, 16
Wynter, John, 76–77

York, House of, 13

Picture Credits

Cover: Old London reconstructed: The Rose Theatre, Southwark (gouache on paper), Jackson, Peter (1922–2003)/Private Collection/© Look and Learn/ Peter Jackson Collection/Bridgeman Images

Maury Aaseng: 14

© Bettmann/CORBIS: 59

© GraphicaArtis/Corbis: 32

© Heritage Images/Corbis: 73, 79

© Lebrecht Music & Arts/Lebrecht Music & Arts/Corbis: 51

© The Print Collector/Corbis: 29

© Joel W. Rogers/CORBIS: 76

© Stapleton Collection/Corbis: 23

Thinkstock Images: 6, 7, 18

Shakespeare performing at the Globe Theatre, Jackson, Peter (1922–2003)/ Private Collection/© Look and Learn/Bridgeman Images: 9

Punishment at school in the Tudor Age (gouache on paper), Jackson, Peter (1922–2003)/Private Collection/© Look and Learn/Bridgeman Images: 36

Inns at the Southwark entrance to London in Shakespeare's time, from 'Inns, Ales, and Drinking Customs of Old England', 1909 (litho), English School, (17th century) (after)/British Library, London, UK/© British Library Board. All Rights Reserved/Bridgeman Images: 44

Elizabethan Townscape (gouache on paper), Doughty, C.L. (1913–85)/ Private Collection/© Look and Learn/Bridgeman Images: 46

Edmund Campion (engraving), English School, (18th century)/Private Collection/Bridgeman Images: 60

Stubbs has his hand cut off, 1521, illustration from 'Hutchinson's Story of the British Nation', c.1923 (litho), Gillett, Frank (1874–1927)/Private Collection/The Stapleton Collection/Bridgeman Images: 67

About the Author

Hal Marcovitz is a former newspaper reporter and columnist. A resident of Chalfont, Pennsylvania, he is the author of more than 170 books for young readers.